THE INTENT OF THE CRITIC

THE INTENT
OF THE CRITIC

BY

Edmund Wilson

Norman Foerster

John Crowe Ransom

W. H. Auden

EDITED, WITH AN INTRODUCTION, BY

Donald A. Stauffer

PRINCETON

PRINCETON UNIVERSITY PRESS

Contents

INTRODUCTION: THE INTENT OF THE CRITIC

By DONALD A. STAUFFER ·

Introduction: The Intent of the Critic

I

"UNDER what circumstances was this work of art created? What did the artist intend to create? How successfully did he accomplish it? By what standards should it be judged? What is its value by these standards?" Such are the questions the critic has learned to ask and answer. They are familiar even to the common readers, among whom, for purposes of this introduction, you and I are two. Since all readers are critics, whether or not they intend to be, informally we ask these questions of ourselves. If they are asked systematically and answered with cool persuasion or warm conviction, we are inclined to think that the job is done. What more can be demanded of the critic? He has redressed some balance, or has made us aware of some element or purpose which the artist embodied in his work, or has aided us in seeing some work of art steadily and whole. We read the essays in this very book, for example, and specific critical comments tell us that Mark Twain's writings may be better understood in the light of a significant childhood incident, or that the poetic value of a song by Shakespeare lies in the interplay of the elements "structure" and "texture," or that Stravinsky and Picasso are typical modern artists because they draw at will from any age and any culture.

Yet we cannot stop here; we cannot accept the critic uncritically. He is a lens through which we see: we should try to be aware of his particular properties.

Let us take a single example. We realize today that we may learn more about Coleridge than about Hamlet when we read Coleridge's words:

"In Hamlet . . . we see a great, an almost enormous, intellectual activity, and a proportionate aversion to real action, consequent upon it, with all its symptoms and accompanying qualities. . . . The effect of this over-balance of the imaginative power is beautifully illustrated in the everlasting broodings and superfluous activities of Hamlet's mind, which, unseated from its healthy relation, is constantly occupied with the world within, and abstracted from the world without,—giving substance to shadows, and throwing a mist over all commonplace actualities. . . . [Hamlet's] senses are in a state of trance, and he looks upon external things as hieroglyphics."

The cat is out of the bag at last when Coleridge confides: "I have a smack of Hamlet myself, if I may say so." Coleridge's remarks, with Goethe's, have shaped the conception of Hamlet's character during the last hundred years, and have made "procrastination" a familiar word in every high school. Coleridge does not illuminate equally and unwaveringly all sections of the play; he turns a glaring spotlight here and there, bringing unnoticed details for the first time into brilliant clarity, and leaving other parts by contrast in even deeper darkness. The spotlight is his own inner light. His opinion is a safe guide, therefore, only if we know Coleridge the critic as well as we know *Hamlet*, the play criticized. Such examples of the necessity of rectifying a critical pronouncement by some inquiry into the critic's character and bias and intention might be multiplied. They show that the question, "What is the intent of the critic?" may be as important to the reading public as the prior question, "What is the intent of the artist?" is to the critic himself.

The title for this gathering of four essays proposes a topic which every year grows in importance. In a simpler world critics had taken for granted that the work of art, like Pallas Athene, had come into being in full maturity. Slowly men became aware that a work of art could not be properly evaluated if it were considered as self-begotten. A poem, a play, is the creation of a particular man living under particular circumstances. Mr. Wilson in his lecture has clearly traced the stirrings of the historical spirit in eighteenth century criticism; and the prevalence of the idea of Original Genius in the eighteenth and nineteenth centuries shows that critics realized more and more that a work of art is individual, unique, the creation of a man.

Even this realization is not enough. If the critic is considered as an interpreter of an artist's work to an audience, then ideally, in order to reach an accurate appraisal, the audience should know not only all it can about the work itself, not only all it can about the artist, but also all it can about the critic and his aims. The new twin goddesses of Psychology and Semantics have made the public more wary in its acceptance of any statement without scrutiny. If we are justified in asking "What was the artist's purpose, and why did he resolve upon it?" we are no less justified in asking "What is the critic's purpose, and why does he hold to it?" Only when we are aware of the relations of artist, work of art, critic, and audience may we be certain that criticism is leading us closer to the actual work of art.

What questions, then, should a reader ask and answer for himself before he trusts this precious and delicate instrument for measuring and weighing which is called the critic?

Every critic is an individual who proposes to act as an interpreter and a systematizer. In the nature of things he must be a single consciousness stimulated by works of art. After he has responded as an individual to a lyric or a tragedy, he becomes a critic professionally when he attempts to act as communicator between art and society. Relative to the artist himself, his methods of communication tend to be rational, systematic, judicial in the application of some standard. The three rôles of the critic—as an individual responding to the work of art, as interpreter to an audience, and finally as judge—merit analysis, for each of them leads to significant corollaries and conclusions.

II

That a work of art is a personal expression is today generally accepted. It is not so widely recognized that literary criticism is also personal expression. A pure literary critic in the actual practice of his profession cannot escape from being an individual excited into a new or an increased awareness by a specific poem or play. The first quality of a literary critic is the natural endowment for responding, intuitively and in his own person, to works of art.

Perhaps this may be stated more clearly in the form of two negative propositions: a critic is not an ideal critic if he thinks of himself as the impersonal voice of truth; neither is he an ideal critic if his primary concern is not the work of art. His interests must be deeply rooted in art itself. If they are not, then he is acting not as a literary critic, but as an observer in some other field who uses literature to furnish illustrations. This distinction is so immediately evident that it need not be labored. We should be on our guard, however, to remember the distinction in practice as well as in theory; in a piece of writing about some book, when we encounter a writer who is primarily or solely the preacher, the politician, the sociologist, the psychologist, the philosopher, the rhetorician, the salesman, the patron, the blood-relative, or the schoolmate, we must recognize him as such. We must not consider him, as he frequently considers himself, a literary critic merely because his subject matter is literature, when his purpose is not criticism of letters. He fails to be a literary critic because his prime interest is not in literature as it exists; his heart is overseas.

Even when he concentrates on the work of art itself the ideal critic does not consider himself an oracle. He recognizes his own human limitations. His generalizations and absolute statements should be considered, both by the critic and by his readers, as aids in understanding, not as eternal laws. Criticism loses its dignity and becomes ridiculous when the critic conceives himself to be an awful tribunal of all the Egyptian gods, before whom the work of art, weighed against a feather in the great scales, is assigned its eschatological deserts. One should not trust too far the powers to read and appraise literature of a critic who feels that after ages of error among multitudes of blind men, he at last has found truth. Much of the criticism put forth by past schools—by the Augustans and the Romantics, by the Parnassians and the Naturalists—fails today to carry as much conviction as it might, simply because a limited or partial position was advanced confidently as sole key and clue to wisdom.

Perhaps we have such schools today. If we have, and if they contain a grain of truth, that truth should not be vitiated by being considered too comprehensive or too absolute. The mode of poetic expression justifies holding infinity in the palm of the hand; the mode of criticism forbids it. The majestic ruins and fragments of past critical systems make it seem that the lovely form of the virgin Truth has been hewn into a thousand pieces, and scattered to the four winds. The good critics have ever been, to continue Milton's images, "the sad friends of Truth, such as durst appear, imitating the careful search that Isis made for the mangled body of Osiris, gathering up limb by limb, still as they could find them." And to any critics or schools of critics who pretend to have discovered all the fragments of Truth, Milton's ringing words still apply:

"We have not yet found them all, Lords and Commons, nor ever shall do, till her Master's second coming."

A critic, then, must not consider his or his school's standards absolute in validity. The assumption of critical infallibility cannot carry universal conviction; among intelligent readers it defeats its own end.

A critic may, of course, be as sharp and simple as he pleases. He may make dogmatic, or unqualified, or general, or absolute statements. Frequently such statements are necessary to get along with an argument, to simplify for the purposes of comprehension; and neatness, clarity, economy, precision are not the least of the critical virtues. But the statements of the ideal critic are working hypotheses made by an individual sensitive to art. They are not impositions upon the universe. In this sense, then, the critic is always conscious of himself as a person. Mr. Auden sets up this standard clearly in his essay when he writes:

"What the critic ought to say is: 'Remember that like you and everyone else I am a weak fallible creature who will often make false judgments; and therefore you must not take everything I say as gospel.' "

Recognizing his own limitations, the critic has the further duty of presenting to himself and to his readers his limited systems and principles as clearly as he can. Mr. Auden, writing of the values which each critic sets up for himself, continues:

"He has a duty in a democracy to tell the public what they are. If I am to trust a reviewer's judgment upon a book I have not read, I want to know among other things his philosophical beliefs."

If a critic makes clear his own position, and from that position gives his view of a work of art in its position, it becomes possible for his reader, from still a third position, to reach some definite conclusions about the work discussed. This kind of mental geometry is essential to the communication of a precise judgment. If you say to me: "My position is 50 feet from you on flat ground. I am six feet high. I am looking upward at an angle of 45 degrees and see the top of a tree directly over your head," I know in consequence that the tree is 56 feet high, a knowledge that would have been impossible without the aid of data concerning your position and observations.

Similarly, after Mr. Wilson in his essay has established his distinction between the standards of experts and the opinion of common readers, he goes on to say:

"You sometimes encounter books that seem to mark precisely the borderline between work that is definitely superior and work that is definitely bad—the novels of John Steinbeck, for example."

Such a remark helps the reader to understand and appreciate Steinbeck; it places Steinbeck because Mr. Wilson has previously established his own position and his own criteria. Because boundaries have been set up, it also helps in judging observations made by other critics: it helps in evaluating and discounting on the one hand journalistic enthusiasts and reforming sociologists, and on the other hand, those men who tend to criticize Steinbeck, or any other artist, by stating in various ways that he is not Dante or Shakespeare.

III

Mr. Wilson's remark about John Steinbeck—and it is only one of many critical judgments incidentally introduced in the following lectures in order to illustrate the general topic of the series—helps the reader to understand or to evaluate an author or a work of art. It illuminates, clarifies, interprets. Though it may be practised for various more specific ends, and though it rarely proposes exhaustive commentary, the intent of all good criticism is in some way to ameliorate the relations between art and its audience.

Is not the work of art self-sufficient? Yes. But it may not be self-explanatory. And the reader may not have the necessary knowledge, or the knack, for full and immediate comprehension. The critic, then, is not trying to improve the work of art, but to improve its auditors, among whom, of course, he may number himself.

Few critics are presumptuous enough to attempt a change in actual extant literature, as Richard Bentley and Nahum Tate corrected their Milton and Shakespeare. Most critics accept the work of art as a *fait accompli*, as something finished and done with and beyond their province to modify.* Judgments of a

* Mr. Centeno, the editor of the previous volume in this series, *The Intent of the Artist*, 1941, distinguishes between *intent*, which may be said roughly to include all relevant happenings in time up to the actual production of a work of art; *content*, which is the fixed (or relatively fixed) work of art itself; and *extent*, which includes all relevant happenings in time after the com-

novel, a picture, or a statue may make it a model or a horrid example, and may therefore influence the development of future works. Such judgments cannot change the actual objectification in time and space which we call the work of art. The reception of a work of art, however, can and usually should be changed. Whole classes of people may be brought up toward its level, or may be kept from blind admiration of an inferior work. Whole nations and ages may be taught to understand other times, other morals; and thus may be guided in translating the alien into what seems the human in terms of their own habits of thought. Criticism, therefore, has genuine usefulness for anyone susceptible to art. In working toward the ideal of a full understanding, none of us is so Olympian as to be above profiting from another's counsel. And out of this reasoning together, the critic and his reader may approach a little nearer to truth, or at any rate, to agreement and to satisfaction.

Le Sacre du printemps or *The Art of the Fugue* is the same succession of sounds, apart from slight or accidental variations, no matter how often we hear it; but we change in relation to it, and may change rapidly toward deeper understanding if we concentrate on

pletion of a work of art. Extent, in other words, since it includes the effects produced by a work of art, therefore includes criticism and the topic of this volume. The main distinction between the intent of the artist and the intent of the critic is that the first is primarily creative, the second primarily analytical.

skilled analyses of what Stravinsky or Bach is achieving in sound. The principle holds in literature. Bradley does not change the text of Shakespeare's four great tragedies in writing about them; he changes the apprehension of their readers. Lowes leaves the "Ancient Mariner" and "Kubla Khan" untouched, but *The Road to Xanadu* is a path of progress on the part of the reader nearer and nearer to the mind of a creative artist. Esthetic criticism perfects the reception of a fixed work of art by increasing the understanding of its recipient. Poem, statue, landscape remain unchanging; but we move toward comprehension if someone explains *what is happening* in those processes of human consciousness generated or symbolized by the works of art themselves. As nearly as possible each of us must experience the original experience which the artist wished to communicate. In this striving toward perfection in communication, each man may of course be his own critic. But without criticism in rudimentary or developed form, self-imposed or gained through the interpreter, the middleman, the professed critic, no understanding is possible.

First of all, the critic-as-interpreter may orient his reader. Presumably every writer knows who he is, where he is, and when he is; ordinarily he does not bother to pass all this information on to the reader, though often it is of extreme importance if the response to a work of art is to parallel or correspond with its creation. A critic may serve the genuinely useful, if humble, purpose of giving the reader program notes, or an introduction. Asserting that the work of art exists as an absolute and supplies all relevant information does not conform with common experience. Pragmatically speaking, whether artist or reader is at fault, frequently a poem or painting falls short in completely conveying all necessary data for its understanding. And ideally speaking it is not the purpose of a work of art to act as formal commentary on itself: ordinarily the footnote, invaluable though it is, is pedestrian, and belongs as a footnote—not interwoven, shall we say, as additional *terza rima* stanzas in the body of the *Divina Commedia*.

A critic, then, may be playing one of his rightful rôles when he says: "This piece was composed by one who fought at Marathon; this by a medieval Christian; this was written to win the favor of Queen Elizabeth; this in a modified ballad stanza; this to be presented at the court of Louis XIV; this to stir up Abolitionist sentiment in the United States of the 1850's; this was completed on a deathbed." In making such statements, however, he is acting as a literary critic only insofar as the facts regarding the artist's purpose, his life, or his background help the reader in understanding and appraising the work. Such remarks as those sketched above constitute the most rudimentary but requisite historical criticism. They relate *relevant* externals to the work of art. The historical scholar may exercise his difficult and precise technique admirably and still never approach criticism. Fundamentally, he acts as a literary critic whenever he makes clear in what manner his discoveries aid in the interpretation of an epic, a short story, or a masque as art.

The critic may also act in rôle if he relates, or calls attention to relationships between, various parts of the work itself considered as self-contained. Here he is simply making explicit what he believes to be implicit in the poem or novel. Explication is not an end in itself; it is a station on the way. It assumes that analysis may help as an intermediate stage in a progress whose goal is a fuller and more immediate apprehension.

Let us imagine, as an example, possible footnotes designed to bring out the meaning of the following stanza from "The Phoenix and the Turtle" by reference solely to the other parts of the poem. They might run:

> "Here the anthem doth commence:
>   Love and constancy *is*[1] dead,
>   *Phoenix*[2] and the *turtle*[3] fled
> In a *mutual flame*[4] from hence."

1. Note the singular verb, which may suggest. . . .

2. Compare, associated with the phoenix, and helping to denote her qualities, such words in the

poem as. . . . Note also the less common conception of the phoenix as feminine.

3. Compare such words and phrases as . . . .

4. Compare, for this idea, and for paradoxical
juxtapositions with opposed ideas, such words
and phrases as . . . .

The full possibilities of the poem considered as
absolute poetry are not realized until all such mental
annotations as far as any intelligent reader can accept
them as legitimately significant, all such comparisons
that tie the whole poem into a unit by mutually illuminating each other, are made, deliberately or unconsciously, for each of the eighteen stanzas.

But for a complete understanding, the poem cannot
stand by itself as an absolute. Its meaning becomes
richer if the reader realizes that Shakespeare made it,
that Shakespeare was an individual who wrote other
poems, and that he did not compose this poem in a
timeless cell insulated from his own characteristic,
habitual thoughts and memories. The critic may help a
reader with notes of this type:

5. *Love and constancy:* For further light on
Shakespeare's relating love and constancy, see
such sonnets as Number CXVI,

"Let me not to the marriage of true minds
Admit impediments. . . ."

Compare also particularly *Romeo and Juliet,*

Othello, Antony and Cleopatra, The Winter's Tale.

The critic may go further. Parallels or varying shades of meaning in the works of contemporaries or of artists of like tempers may make more precise the thought expressed in the poem. Shakespeare uses the word "true" in this poem (as, indeed, he uses it elsewhere) more to suggest eternal loyalty inspired by love than to suggest the *veritas* of the philosophers. A critic, and a reader, might find that the following note made the poem more significant:

6. *Truth:* Compare John Donne's "The Dreame," the entire poem, but especially in the first stanza the lines:

"Thou art so truth, that thoughts of thee suffice
To make dreames truths; and fables histories."

Such notes as these could be expanded into a connected essay. Many modern critical writings actually fall into this form. All of the ideas specified may be related by logic, by discursive reasoning. Any part of the poem may be enriched and clarified by comparisons with ideas contained elsewhere within the single poem, or by parallels in other works by Shakespeare himself, or by ideas in the works of his contemporaries, predecessors, and followers. The contents of at least the first four notes were presumably present in the mind of Shakespeare when he wrote the poem, and their relationship, plus all similar relationships within the poem itself, account for the sense of unity in complexity which is one of the marks of poetry.

It is inconceivable that an artist *as artist* should put such appendages within his poem. Part of his function must be to maintain its unity of effect. But the reader must also achieve the complexity of the artist's original vision. The critic may help him to grasp and relate these complex elements by pointing to them. Criticism thus becomes, in one of its typical functions, the use of discursive reason in order more nearly to approximate the original intuition. The critic as an individual *begins* by responding to a work of art, and this response is intuitive, immediate, natural. But in his second rôle as interpreter he *continues* by analyzing, explaining, enlarging upon, scrutinizing his own original, pleasurable, intuitive apprehension. As Mr. Foerster says, a critic not only "feels" a book; he also "thinks" it. To a public lacking time, knowledge, equipment, or insight, the critic can make explicit in public terms what is implicit in the particular and local work of art. The critic in this regard, then, might be compared to an Old French scholar who explains to us the meaning of certain words or lines in the *Chanson de Roland*: without changing the French text, but with the use of circumlocutions, equivalents, comparisons, alternatives, and hypotheses, he changes us, "improves" us, so that we are closer to an expressive mind, in France, in the Middle Ages. In his rôle as interpreter, the critic expatiates; he establishes relationships; he makes references clear; he sets a poem in its context historical, biographical, and artistic.

IV

Relative to the work of art, this process of criticism-as-explanation is rational and systematic. The critic makes a statement and proceeds to illustrate it; in most great works of art statement and illustration are not distinguished from each other. Genuine criticism is always a transposition of the work of art into different, more systematic, terms. The creative artist modifying his work as he proceeds is striving always toward producing a perfect work of art, which, briefly, might be defined as a work in which complex elements fuse to produce a sense of instantaneous or continuous organic unity. No pure work of art, therefore, is a succession of articulated philosophical arguments. This truth, so evident in music, painting, and the plastic arts, is often forgotten in literature because its raw materials—words —possess conceptual significance. In the intent of his creations, the literary artist belongs near the angelic order: his intelligence (at least his mode of expression) is marked by intuitive rather than by discursive reason. Discursive thoughts may have entered into his creation;

but the whole effect of the finished work of art as art is that of a single immediate intuition. In making it comprehensible to the ordinary reader, who almost certainly is not living in a state of inspiration, the critic therefore must usually translate its flash of insight back into the light of common day by utilizing the resources of discursive reasoning.

This translation, which is the method, may be performed for various ends. To accomplish such translation without assuming or announcing certain standards is extremely difficult, for standards exist even in the simple form of categories for discourse. In the first four footnotes to "The Phoenix and the Turtle," for example, the category of the word as opposed to the whole poem was assumed to have validity: separate words were compared, were regarded one by one as if they had existence independent from their unique articulation in a unique poem. And in the four essays that follow, none of the critics proceeds even to a first sentence without setting up standards and beliefs, so that we might guess from the titles that Mr. Wilson's standards are historical, Mr. Ransom's metaphysical, Mr. Foerster's esthetic and ethical, Mr. Auden's sociological.

If the critic-as-individual responds directly to a poem, sets up his own stand, and realizes his own limitations (which in itself implies awareness of standards), and if the critic-as-interpreter tries to bring together more closely the reader and the work of art, the critic-as-systematizer must measure the work of art in important respects. Ultimately, since the very word "important" requires a value-judgment, he must determine the worth of his material. To accomplish this, he *must* set up certain standards not formally expressed within the work of art, for no great book judges itself, and no judgment can be made without some standard, some code or decalogue or yardstick. The responsible critic cannot present such a final judgment in a flash. A great work of art is so complex that a simple evaluation may easily be false. And if a poem is so difficult that a reader cannot appraise it completely with ease and speed, then the process of ameliorating the relationship between reader and poem must proceed slowly and partially. One thing must be considered at a time. The very word criticism, deriving ultimately from a Greek verb meaning to separate, suggests that the natural, perhaps the inevitable, method of criticizing is to consider separable parts or elements in a poem or picture. And when the critic separates parts from a whole novel or drama, the critic will be tending toward judgments regarding values. He will be stating, or implying, that the diction of a poem, the structure of a play, the social ideas of a novel, the use of sources in an epic, the moral profundity of an artist, are worth serious consideration.

The "compleat critick" will strive to see that his various parts or separations, necessary for analysis and simple communication, are related, and that taken together they make a sum that approximates the whole. He will realize that the methods of analysis, however, are not the equivalent of the direct, intuitive apprehension that constitutes esthetic pleasure; and that the sum of his systematized topics and observations can never be completely equal to the original imaginative creation. The ideal critic should also be aware, and should make his readers aware, of what he is not considering, but what should be considered in any total criticism; he should examine and answer the questions: how and why his particular standards are valid and applicable to the art considered, what their relation is to the work of art in itself, and what changes or possible distortions in comprehending the work of art the application of his standards may be effecting. In a sense he will use the work of art as a standard by means of which he judges the validity and efficacy of his own principles. And here again he will be returning to his original intuitive response. In the ideal critic, the three rôles which this introduction has sought to make distinct actually tend to coalesce, or at least to supplement each other in the final effectiveness of his criticism.

Insistence upon discursive thought, logical analysis, clear statements, and systematization up to this point in the introduction does not indicate that the critic believes that art is wholly or chiefly rational. Reason may be aware that it must reconstruct and restate the actuality and totality of a work of art by reference to, or awareness of, forms of consciousness other than reason itself. Nevertheless, in being aware of such distinctions, critical *theory* still remains rational and systematic. Even when he is dealing with the most intractable and irrational material, the critic maintains his systematic approach. Though the roads lead to strange countries like Xanadu and Tryermaine, critics will erect signposts and arrows along the paths. Freudianism deals with the subconscious; but literary criticism on Freudian grounds is conscious criticism, and handles with some system the patterns and types which psychologists have established. Semantics considers the shifting and multiple meanings of words, but semantic criticism strives to give clear outlines to the amorphous; if we are dealing with ambiguity, let us at least have seven types of ambiguity.

The human mind will not easily or for long put up with the indefinite, the imprecise, and the shapeless. All men crave forms and standards. We take delight in recognition. The individual work of art has precision in itself; the critic must make equally precise the relations, as he sees them, between the work of art and its various elements, its milieu, its history, its creator, its reader, its critic, and all standards used in judging it.

The critic keeps a perilous balance between awareness of the individual work of art and awareness of its communal audience. Unique, extrarational in many of its elements, and immediate as a poem is and must, after criticism, remain, the critic must nevertheless proceed *in method* to find in it common elements which may make it more intelligible after deliberate survey and analysis. And finally, no man is a literary critic, excellent though he be as esthetician, scholar, or creative artist, in whose writings our primary pleasure does not spring from seeing specific works of art more clearly, easily, or completely.

V

The critics whose essays are published in this volume do not represent a single point of view. Some of them could not easily be attached to any school at all. Collaboration in this symposium has not gone beyond the bounds of sending to each of the writers brief and imperfect abstracts of each of the other three essays; if the issues do not join perfectly, or if there has been any misunderstanding of what was said by the other contributors to the series, the fault lies in the roughness of these transcripts. Each man developed his subject as he pleased, with no limitation other than the general topic of the symposium. They represent, perhaps as well as any four writers could represent, a cross-section of critical opinion in America today.

A few preliminary analyses might indicate how the essays supplement, oppose, or reinforce each other, what topics or problems arise more than once, and what accord exists in considering the functions of the literary critic. Agreement on the answers to critical questions may not be so important as agreement on what questions should be asked; it would seem a better state of affairs if all critics naturally faced the same essential questions, whatever their solutions, just as it seems more orderly and sensible to assume that men enter a polling-booth in order to vote, rather than to suppose that Smith enters because he likes to make X's on paper, Brown in order to please his wife, and Jones because he wishes to be alone.

These four essays fall into numerous balances and counter-balances. Mr. Wilson and Mr. Auden, for example, develop their arguments historically. Mr. Wilson shows criticism as a branch of the history of ideas, its manner and even its content changing with the decades. Mr. Auden also considers criticism a function of society, and sees the critic, in one aspect at least, as a corpuscle in the body politic: as the state changes, so does the literary critic. To this extent, then, both Mr. Wilson and Mr. Auden are relativists. Mr. Foerster and Mr. Ransom are more nearly absolute. For Mr. Foerster, literary criticism must combine esthetic and ethical judgment; he demands belief from the critic and does not beg the issue by suggesting finally that one man may believe all things; he is definite and consistent in his judgment that today, after our "return to Nature," we need a "return to Man." Mr. Ransom, on the other hand, leaves moral judgments to moralists, and focusses on the metaphysics of poetry. His ideal critic must have conscious esthetic standards; and Mr. Ransom sets up for him, in systematic philosophical speculations, a conception of the essence of art.

One might feel that lines are sharply drawn between Mr. Foerster and Mr. Ransom, and that the venerable issues of form versus content, of art-as-manner versus art-as-matter are not yet finally settled. Indeed, such problems occupy to a considerable extent the two middle essays of this volume; and part of the reader's pleasure in them derives from the cogency and the confidence with which the two divergent positions are stated. But, even more interesting, in these two essays as well as in the other two, modern criticism avoids the merely mechanical and doctrinaire. It is continuously aware of larger frames; it repeatedly points out the dangers of limited systems. Thus Mr. Foerster, in spite of his decided ethical convictions, insists that the ethical judgment must be coupled with the esthetic judgment to form valid literary criticism, points to the Neo-Humanist weakness in neglecting esthetic criticism, and speaks of the "heresy" of didacticism unsupported by esthetics. And Mr. Ransom is equally careful to point out that Art for Art's Sake, a doctrine with which the unwary might suspect him to sympathize, is empty, vapid, and inadequate, imputing less positive substance to poetry than does moralistic criticism. To-day, then, even coherent and exclusive systems demand a balanced judgment, an awareness of other possible coherent and exclusive systems, and a consciousness of the relation of one's own system to larger structures.

All four contributors seem in agreement as to the distinction between esthetics and literary criticism, that is, between a philosophy and its application. Few statements or arguments are allowed to pass in these lectures unsupported by illustrations; for the writers are too well aware in their own practice of the value and difficulty of literary judgments to build up rules and theories supposedly applicable to criticism but actually untested by experience. The general topic of the series lends itself readily to esthetic speculation, and it is of particular importance, therefore, that no one of the writers has been willing to stop with esthetics alone. As Mr. Ransom suggests, literary criticism may profit from greater introspection; similarly, literary esthetics will certainly profit if, as in this series, practising literary critics give their answers to its problems on the basis of their experience.

Again, all four writers agree upon the need for standards that are workable yet high and exacting enough to compel the allegiance of intelligent people. The essays are at their best, their most exciting and their most serious, in this quest for critical standards— in Mr. Wilson's closely reasoned, deceptively simple final pages, in Mr. Foerster's extended argument relating the great tradition to the present day, in Mr. Ransom's gradual revelation of the metaphysical bases for art, in Mr. Auden's historical survey and analysis of the beliefs underlying past critical systems and his formulation of the critic's duties today and tomorrow. In each of the four essays there are notable remarks on the relation between belief and criticism, the problem which is not only the most vexing but probably the most vital to the criticism of our time.

A question that has troubled the waters considerably in the last decade has been the relation between literature and propaganda. On this topic the four critics are not voluble. Mr. Foerster specifically states that literary criticism is not concerned with ulterior effects. Mr. Wilson shows clearly and for the first time how art-as-propaganda became mixed with Marxism because of their accidental flourishing together in Russia. By implication in all the essays, the aim of art is not to propagandize. Art is contemplative rather than hortatory: Mr. Wilson submits art and criticism to the pragmatic test, it is true, but the test is that art and criticism must give *meaning* to experience; the contemplative moral basis in art and criticism is sufficiently evident in both Mr. Foerster and Mr. Auden; and when Mr. Ransom speaks of possible ethical content in a poem, he finds there composure, not incitement to action, "as if the poet had long known good and evil, and made his moral choice between them once and for all." If we may trust our four critics, therefore, the world need not worry in the immediate future over the bluff, blunt, and rather stupid question as to whether or not the poet and dramatist and novelist are duty bound to enter the world of practical action and propaganda.

There is agreement also that criticism is necessarily becoming more complex and difficult. Mr. Wilson's essay is a leisurely exposition of this growing complexity; Mr. Foerster and Mr. Ransom meet it by seeking to make the critic more effective as a specialist in definite fields; Mr. Auden details the critic's duties in the cross-currents of new and complex societies. One cannot read these four essays and feel blithely that criticism is a frivolous, pleasing, and unimportant game; it is no such pastime as the textual emendation of Mr. Housman's scholiast, like leaning against a wall, and spitting.

How seriously these essayists conceive the rôle of the critic may be deduced from the little they have to say about book reviewing. The influence of the book review in the daily paper, the Sunday supplement, or the popular periodical is one of the most striking developments of modern literature. Possibly such book reviewing merits the attention of the expert on public opinion, the sociologist, or even the economist, rather than that of the literary critic. Certainly our lecturers agree to ignore it, with the exception of Mr. Auden, who treats journalistic criticism as a sociologist. He is alive to the power of such popular criticism in shaping the taste and the reading habits of great masses of citizens; and, aware of the power of the journalists, he is likewise aware of their responsibilities, and expresses some serious thoughts on this relatively neglected theme.

On the whole, these essays are not astonishingly topical. There is not as much evidence as one might expect, for instance, that they were written during a time of crisis and world conflict. Of the two historical critics, Mr. Wilson has almost completely excluded reference to immediate and quotidian topics; Mr. Auden has developed a comprehensive view of the relation between society and the critic, and in the application of his principles to literary criticism today in America, has written an eloquent manifesto supporting the democratic and Christian as against the totalitarian way of life. Mr. Foerster is also aware of the close connection between current beliefs and a vital criticism, and his paper comes to its climax and conclusion in considering the significance today of such traditional phrases as freedom of the spirit and the dignity of man. Mr. Ransom takes advantage of our present consciousness of democracy and totalitarianism to build one of his most illuminating comparisons. In the main the tyranny of the immediate and the topical has not here affected the constructive and permanent interests of criticism.

We have here no Scotch reviewers like Jeffrey, no critic-as-dictator like Doctor Johnson or Matthew Arnold. Evidently the critic today is not a welfare-worker whose business is the reformation of the artist. These men do not lecture the artist, as if the critic were superior by nature to the creative writer.

VI

Perhaps the most vexing question which these four essays raises is that of the proper domain of literary criticism. Setting the bounds is not just an exercise in ingenuity; it is of importance, for the range of the literary critic—how far he travels before he believes he has gone astray—will partially determine his purpose. Of the four writers represented in this volume, the one who interprets criticism in the widest sense, Mr. Auden, draws incidental illustrations from many forms of art and of mental activity (indeed, in his own poetry psychologists and anthropologists appear as easily as pure men of letters) ; while the one who sets strictest bounds on criticism, Mr. Ransom, tends to limit literary criticism even more strictly to the consideration of poetry alone. Literature, though it is a way of writing, must write about something. A man of letters may write about anything. Since literature has no proper subject matter, Mr. Ransom leans toward the assumption that the literary critic should disregard all subject matter as irrelevant to his profession, whereas Mr. Auden, on the same premise, tends toward the antithetical conclusion that no subject matter written is alien to the literary critic. I am making this opposition too simple and too extreme, I know; but Mr. Auden and Mr. Ransom are perfectly able to take care of themselves, and their two essays illustrate strikingly how diverse are the opinions on the proper scope of literary criticism. Mr. Auden, of course, proceeds as an anthropologist, Mr. Ransom as a philosopher; but the startling point here is the difference in *range* between them.

I have no intention of stepping in between the fell-incensèd points of mighty opposites. Though I share Monsieur Jourdain's delight in listening to disputing experts, I do not wish to play his rôle in minimizing differences of opinion by saying, *Vous avez raison tous deux*. Nor do I subscribe to the naïve conviction that criticism would profit if all critics would make up their minds to believe the same thing, or failing that, would at least clean up current confusion by jointly defining their terms and holding to their joint definitions. Literary criticism would indeed be in a bad way if some Académie Américaine defined for all time classicism, and tragedy, and realism, and imagination, and organic unity, and finally criticism and the intent of the critic. Such attempts prefer certainty and finality to experience; they prefer clarity in a philosophical construction to clarity in a work of art and fidelity in the critic who appraises it. This is not precision, but rigidity.

Nevertheless, sharp lines of thought in each individual critic help others to set up sharp lines in their own systems of judgments. The air is cleared when Mr. Ransom writes: "In strictness, the business of the literary critic is exclusively with an esthetic criticism." Since the days of Kant, notably since the days of Benedetto Croce, such a belief has worked wonders in the actual practice of literary criticism. By limiting the field for the critic and by setting him a definite task, much irrelevant and confused material has been eliminated, and many detailed contributions to critical knowledge have been made. Because of numerous specific analyses based on the principle which Mr. Ransom here enunciates, the world is today in a much better position to realize the distinctive qualities of art.

The clear statement of the doctrine that literary criticism is exclusively esthetic is of value to all critics, therefore, whether or not their own doctrines support it. Clarity, conviction, singleness of purpose, continuity in maintaining a doctrine, at last make it necessary for all theorists, even when unsympathetic, to take it into account in developing their own systems. Thanks

to critics like Mr. Ransom, for instance, no one of the
other writers in this volume neglects, or could have
afforded to neglect, esthetic criticism. Mr. Wilson cannot end his essay on the historical aspects of criticism
without serious consideration of the distinctive qualities of literature. Mr. Auden throughout his essay assumes the critic's primary awareness of esthetic values.
Mr. Foerster takes the most conservative position expressed in these lectures. No one would mistake him
for a pure esthetic critic. He believes that art aims
at wisdom as well as delight. Yet though he believes
this firmly and defends it staunchly, he is no less aware
of the necessity for esthetic criticism, and he reveals,
as a critic in the great tradition could not have revealed
a few decades ago, the weaknesses and blindnesses
and lack of esthetic sensitivity of those very Neo-
Humanistic critics with whom he most naturally sym-
pathizes.

The boundaries of criticism, then, cannot be fixed
by any accord unanimously agreed upon by the writers
of the four ensuing essays. Mr. Ransom limits himself
to esthetics; Mr. Foerster, including esthetics, nevertheless focusses on ethics, in the sense of contemplative
wisdom for the individual, largely as determined by the
tested standards of the past; Mr. Wilson substitutes
the present for the past, and adds to the esthetic and
ethical judgment the social standard as well, introduc-
ing all the complexities which an awareness of society

may make in any appraisal of literature; Mr. Auden accepts all these standards, assumes the necessity for Mr. Wilson's complex sociological criteria, is acutely aware of contemporaneity, but at the same time reintroduces the past as a necessary part of a continually modified tradition.

The relation of literary criticism to life and society, its wider orientation, is significant; and in essays like Mr. Auden's and Mr. Wilson's, historically and socially centered, this relation is never far from their thought. Mr. Foerster also realizes its importance: in speaking of such men as More and Babbitt he even attributes their failure to produce much great esthetic criticism to the Neo-Humanist belief that the moral and social implications of literature, the relations of literature to life, are of prime importance. To such comprehensive appraisals, which insist upon seeing literature as part of larger movements of thought, Mr. Foerster gives the name of "general criticism"; and of such general criticism Mr. Auden's essay in large measure would be an example.

VII

On the basis of these four essays, if one might generalize concerning the future of criticism, two observations might be justifiable. First, the increasing complexity of criticism has also increased its competence. We have here the work of experts. They have made themselves experts, because as the problems of criticism became more difficult, the necessity arose to develop the instruments of experts in order to criticize at all. Second, criticism without some system and some belief is empty. The beliefs, whatever they are and may be, must remain elastic, capable of adaptation and modification; system is required, but does not imply ossification; tolerance is required, but it must not serve as a cloak for agnosticism. The critic perpetually walks the knife-edge between a sterile dogma and a sterile skepticism. He may say with Robert Bridges:

"Our stability is but balance, and conduct lies
     in masterful administration of the unforeseen."

The following four essays are parts of a varied unity. They hold without exception to literary criticism, yet each has its own flavor, and the four seem serially to have been written by an historian, a traditional moralist, a metaphysician, and an educator. If these catchwords are descriptively accurate, then the writers have the ability to escape from themselves or their professional environment and to don Yeatsian masks. For the historian is Mr. Wilson, one of the editors of the *New Republic* and a distinguished critic in such esoteric fields as modern symbolism. The traditional moralist is Mr. Foerster who at the University of Iowa heads one of the most important experiments in this nation toward making creative as well as critical activity a part of our system of higher learning. The metaphysician is Mr. Ransom, a notable poet in his own right, editor of the *Kenyon Review*, and a professor of literature. And the man who makes such an eloquent plea for the value and power of education in a democracy is Mr. Auden, who in his poems, as if to exemplify Shelley's poet as prophet, moves in the vanguard of contemporary thought.

THE HISTORICAL INTERPRETATION
OF LITERATURE

· By EDMUND WILSON ·

The Historical Interpretation of Literature

I WANT to talk about the historical interpretation of literature—that is, about the interpretation of literature in its social, economic and political aspects.

To begin with, it will be worth while to say something about the kind of criticism which seems to be furthest removed from this. There is a kind of comparative criticism which tends to be non-historical. The essays of T. S. Eliot, which have had such an immense influence in our time, are, for example, fundamentally non-historical. Eliot sees, or tries to see, the whole of literature, so far as he is acquainted with it, spread out before him under the aspect of eternity. He then compares the work of different periods and countries, and tries to draw from it general conclusions about what literature ought to be. He understands, of course, that our point of view in connection with literature changes, and he has what seems to me a very sound conception of the whole body of writing of the past as something to which new works are continually being added, and which is not merely increased in bulk thereby but modified as a whole—so that Sophocles is no longer precisely what he was for

Aristotle, or Shakespeare what he was for Ben Jonson or for Dryden or for Dr. Johnson, on account of all the later literature that has intervened between them and us. Yet at every point of this continual accretion, the whole field may be surveyed, as it were, spread out before the critic. The critic tries to see it as God might: he calls the books to a Day of Judgment. And looking at things in this way, he may arrive at interesting and valuable conclusions which could hardly be reached by approaching them in any other way. Eliot was able to see, for example—what I believe had never been noticed before—that the French symbolist poetry of the nineteenth century had certain fundamental resemblances to the English poetry of the age of Donne. Another kind of critic would draw certain historical conclusions from these purely esthetic findings, as the Russian D. S. Mirsky did; but Eliot does not draw them.

Another example of this kind of non-historical criticism, in a somewhat different way and on a somewhat different plane, is the work of the late George Saintsbury. Saintsbury was a connoisseur of wines; he wrote an entertaining book on the subject. And his attitude toward literature, too, was that of the connoisseur. He tastes the authors and tells you about the vintages; he distinguishes the qualities of the various wines. His palate was as fine as could be, and he possessed the great qualification that he knew how to take books on their own terms and was thus able to appreciate a very large variety of different kinds of writing. He was a man of strong social prejudices and peculiarly intransigent political views, but, so far as it is humanly possible, he kept them out of his literary criticism. The result is one of the most agreeable commentaries on literature that have ever been written. Most scholars who have read as much as Saintsbury don't have Saintsbury's discriminating taste. Saintsbury has been over the whole ground like any academic historian; but his account of it is not merely a chronology: it is a record of fastidious enjoyment. Since enjoyment is the only thing he is looking for, he does not need to know the causes of things, and the historical background of literature does not interest him very much.

There is, however, another tradition of criticism that dates from the beginning of the eighteenth century. In 1725, the Neapolitan philosopher Vico published *La Scienza Nuova*, a revolutionary work on the philosophy of history, in which he asserted for the first time that *the social world* was *certainly the work of man*, and attempted what is, so far as I know, the first social interpretation of a work of literature. This is what Vico says about Homer: "Homer composed the *Iliad in his youth*—that is, in the youth of Greece. Greece was then all aflame with sublime passions, with pride, anger and vengeance. These sentiments are incompatible with dissimulation and do not exclude generosity; Greece admired Achilles, *the hero of force.* Homer composed the *Odyssey* when he was *old,* when the passions of the Greeks were beginning to be cooled by reflection, the mother of prudence. Greece now admired Ulysses, *the hero of prudence.* In the time of Homer's youth, the pride of Agamemnon, the insolence and barbarity of Achilles, were what was pleasing to the peoples of Greece. In the time of its old age, they already liked the luxury of Alcinoüs, the delights of Calypso, the sensuous pleasures of Circe, the songs of the sirens, and the pastimes of the lovers of Penelope. How could one possibly assign to the same age manners so completely dissimilar? Plato is so much impressed by this difficulty that, not knowing how to resolve it, he pretends that in his divine transports of poetic enthusiasm, Homer was able to foresee the effeminate and dissolute life of the future. But isn't this to attribute the height of imprudence to him whom he presents as the founder of Greek civilization? To publish an account of such manners before they existed, even though one condemned them at the same time, wouldn't this be to teach people to imitate them? Let us agree rather that the author of the *Iliad* must have long preceded the author of the *Odyssey*—that the former, who came from the northeastern part of Greece, sang of the Trojan War, which had taken place in his part of the country; whereas the latter, who had been born in the southeastern part, celebrated Ulysses, who reigned in that part of the world."

You see that Vico has here explained Homer in terms both of historical period and of geographical origin. The idea that human arts and institutions were to be studied and elucidated as the products of the geographical and climatic conditions in which the people who created them lived and of the phase of their social development through which they were passing at the moment, made great progress during the eighteenth century. There are traces of it even in Dr. Johnson, that most orthodox and classical of critics—as, for example, when he accounts for certain characteristics of Shakespeare by the relative barbarity of the age in which he lived, pointing out just as Vico had done that "nations, like individuals, have their infancy." And by the eighties of the eighteenth century Herder, in his *Ideas on the Philosophy of History*, was writing of poetry that it was a kind of "Proteus among the people, which is always changing its form in response to the languages, manners and habits, to the temperaments and climates, nay, even to the accents of different nations." He said—what could still seem startling even so late as that—that "language was not a divine communication, but something men had produced themselves." In the lectures on the philosophy of history that Hegel delivered in Berlin in 1822-1823, he discussed the national literatures as expressions of the societies which had produced them—societies which he conceived as great organisms continually transforming themselves under the propulsion of a succession of dominant ideas.

In the field of literary criticism, this historical point of view came to its first complete flower in the work of the French critic Taine, in the middle of the nineteenth century. The whole school of historian-critics to which he belonged—Michelet, Renan, Sainte-Beuve—had been occupied in interpreting books in terms of their historical origins. But Taine was the first to try to apply these principles systematically and on a large scale to a work devoted exclusively to literature. In the Introduction to his *History of English Literature*, published in 1863, he made his famous pronouncement that works of literature were to be understood as the upshot of three interfusing factors: *the moment, the race, and the milieu.* Taine thought he was a scientist and a mechanist who was examining works of literature from the same point of view as the chemist in experimenting with chemical compounds. But the difference between the critic and the chemist is that the critic cannot first combine his elements and then watch to see what they will do: he can only examine phenomena which have already taken place. What Taine actually does is pretend to set the stage for the experiment by describing the moment, the race,and the milieu; and then say, "Such a situation demands such a kind of writer." He now goes on to describe the kind of writer that the situation demands, and at the end of the description we discover that we are confronted with Shakespeare or Milton or Byron, or whoever the great figure is—who turns out to prove the accuracy of Taine's prognosis by precisely fitting the description.

There is thus an element of imposture in Taine; but it is a lucky thing that there is. If he had really been the mechanist that he thought he was, his work on literature would have had little value. The truth was that Taine loved literature for its own sake—he was at his best an excellent artist himself—and that he had very strong moral convictions which give his writing emotional power. His mind, to be sure, was an analytic one, and his analysis, though terribly oversimplified, does have an explanatory value. Yet his work was what we call creative. Whatever he may say about chemical experiments, it is evident when he writes of a great writer that the moment, the race and the milieu have combined, like the three sounds of the chord in Browning's poem about Abt Vogler, to produce not a fourth sound but a star.

To Taine's set of elements was added, dating from the middle of the century, a new element, the economic, which was introduced into the discussion of historical phenomena mainly by Marx and Engels. The non-Marxist critics themselves were at the time already taking into account the influence of the social classes. In his chapters on the Norman conquest of England, Taine shows that the difference between the literatures produced respectively by the Normans and the Saxons was partly the difference between a ruling class, on the one hand, and a vanquished and oppressed class, on the other. And Michelet in his volume on the Regency, which was finished the same year that the *History of English Literature* appeared, studies *Manon Lescaut* as a document representing the point of view of the small gentry before the French Revolution. But Marx and Engels derived the social classes from the ways that people made or got their livings— from what they called the *methods of production;* and they tended to regard these economic processes as fundamental to civilization.

The Dialectical Materialism of Marx and Engels was not really so materialistic as it sounds. There was in it a large element of the Hegelian idealism that Marx and Engels thought they had gotten rid of. At no time did they take so mechanistic a view of things as Taine began by professing; and their theory of the relation of works of literature to what they called the *economic base* was a good deal less simple than Taine's theory of the moment, the race and the milieu. They thought that art, politics, religion, philosophy and literature belonged to what they called the *super-*

structure of human activity; but they saw that the practitioners of these various departments tended also to
constitute social groups, and that they were always pull-
ing away from the kind of solidarity based on economic
classes in order to establish a professional solidarity of
their own. Furthermore, the activities of the superstruc-
ture could influence one another, and they could influence the economic base. It may be said of Marx and
Engels in general that, contrary to the popular impression, they were modest, confused and groping, where a
materialist like Taine was cocksure. Marx once made
an attempt to explain why the poems of Homer were
so good when the society that produced them was from
his point of view—that is, from the industrial point of
view—so primitive; and this gave him a good deal of
trouble. If we compare his discussion of this problem
with Vico's discussion of Homer, we see that the explanation of literature in terms of a philosophy of social
history is becoming, instead of simpler and easier, more
difficult and complex.

Marx and Engels were deeply imbued, moreover,
with the German admiration for literature which they
had learned from the age of Goethe. It would never
have occurred to either of them that *der Dichter* was
not one of the noblest and most beneficent of human-
kind. When Engels writes about Goethe, he presents
him as a man equipped for "practical life," whose career

was frustrated by the "misery" of the historical situation in Germany in his time, and reproaches him for allowing himself to lapse into the "cautious, smug and narrow" philistinism of the class from which he came; but Engels regrets this because it interfered with the development of the "mocking, defiant, world-despising genius," "*der geniale Dichter*," "*der gewaltige Poet*," of whom Engels would not even, he says, have asked that he should have been a political liberal if he had not sacrificed to his bourgeois shrinkings his truer esthetic sense. And the great critics who were trained on Marx—Franz Mehring and Bernard Shaw—had all this reverence for the priesthood of literature. Shaw deplores the lack of political philosophy and what he regards as the middle-class snobbery in Shakespeare; but he celebrates Shakespeare's poetry and his dramatic imagination almost as enthusiastically as Swinburne did, describing even those pot-boiling comedies— *Twelfth Night* and *As You Like It*—the themes of which seem to him most contemptible, as "the Crown Jewels of English dramatic poetry." Such a critic may do more for a writer by showing him a real man in a real world at a definite moment of time than the impressionist critic of Swinburne's type who flourished in the same period of the late nineteenth century. The purely impressionist critic approaches the whole of literature as an exhibit of bellettristic jewels, and he can only write a rhapsodic catalogue. But when Shaw turned his spotlight on Shakespeare as a figure in the Shavian drama of history, he invested him with a new interest as perhaps no other English critic had done.

The insistence that the man of letters should play a political rôle, the disparagement of works of art in comparison with political action, were thus originally no part of Marxism. They only became associated with it later. This happened by way of Russia, and it was due to special tendencies in that country that date from long before the Revolution or the promulgation of Marxism itself. In Russia there have been very good reasons why the political implications of literature should particularly occupy the critics. The art of Pushkin itself, with its marvellous power of implication, had certainly been partly created by the censorship of Nicholas I, and Pushkin set the tradition for most of the great Russian writers that followed him. Every play, every poem, every story, must be a parable of which the moral is implied. If it were stated, the censor would suppress the book, as he tried to do with *The Bronze Horseman* of Pushkin, where it was merely a question of the packed implications protruding a little too plainly. Right down through the writings of Chekhov and up almost to the Revolution, the imaginative literature of Russia presents the peculiar paradox of an art which is technically objective and yet charged with dynamic social messages. In Russia under the Tsar, all social criticism was necessarily political because the most urgent need from the point of view of the intelligentsia was to get rid of the Tsarist régime. Even the neo-Christian moralist Tolstoy, who pretends to be non-political, is as political in his implications as any because his preaching will inevitably embroil him with the Church, and the Church is an integral part of the tsardom. His pamphlet called *What Is Art?*, in which he throws overboard Shakespeare and a large part of modern literature, including his own novels, in the interests of his intransigent morality, is the example which is most familiar to us of the moralizing Russian criticism; but it was only the most sensational expression of a kind of approach which had been prevalent since Belinsky and Chernyshevsky in the early part of the century. The critics, who were usually journalists writing in exile or in a contraband press, were always tending to demand of the imaginative writers that they should illustrate bolder morals.

After the Revolution occurred, this situation did not change. The old habits of censorship persisted in the new socialist society of the Soviets, which was necessarily made up of people who had been stamped by the die of the old despotism. We find the peculiar phenom-

enon of a series of literary groups attempting one after
another to obtain official recognition or to make themselves sufficiently powerful so that they could establish
themselves are arbiters of literature. Lenin and Trotsky
and Lunacharsky had the sense to oppose these attempts: the comrade-dictators of Proletcult or Lev or
Rapp would certainly have been just as bad as the
Count Benckendorf who made Pushkin miserable, and
when the Stalin bureaucracy, after the death of Gorky,
got control of this department as of everything else,
they instituted a system of repression that made Benckendorf and Nicholas I look like Lorenzo de' Medici. In
the meantime, Trotsky, himself a great political writer
who had always had an interest in belles-lettres, attempted in 1924, apropos of one of these movements,
to clarify the situation. He wrote a brilliant and important book called *Literature and Revolution*, in
which he explained the aims of the government, ana-
lysed the work of the Russian writers, and praised or
rebuked the latter as they seemed to him in harmony
or in conflict with the former. Trotsky is intelligent,
sympathetic; it is evident that he is really fond of
literature and that he knows that a work of art does
not fulfil its function in terms of the formulas of party
propaganda. But Mayakovsky, the Soviet poet, whom
Trotsky had praised with reservations, expressed himself in a famous joke when he was asked what he
thought about Trotsky's book—a pun which implied

that a Commissar turned critic was unmistakably a Commissar still; and what a foreigner cannot accept in Trotsky is his assumption that it is the duty of the government to take a hand in the direction of literature.

This point of view, indigenous to Russia, has been imported to other countries through the permeation of Communist influence. The Communist press and its literary followers have reflected the control of the Kremlin in all the phases through which it has passed, down to the wholesale imprisonment of Soviet writers which has been taking place since 1935. But it has never been a part of the American system that our Republican or Democratic administration should lay down a political line for the guidance of the national literature. A gesture in this direction lately on the part of Archibald MacLeish, who seems a little carried away by the eminence of his position as Librarian of Congress, was anything but cordially received by serious American writers. And so long as the United States happily remains a non-totalitarian country, we can very well do without this aspect of the historical criticism of literature.

Another element of a different order has, however, since Marx's time been added to the historical study of the origins of works of literature. I mean the psychoanalysis of Freud. This appears as an extension of something which had already got well started before, which had figured even in Johnson's *Lives of the Poets*, and of which the great exponent had been Sainte-Beuve: the interpretation of works of literature in the light of the personalities behind them. But the Freudians made this interpretation more exact and more systematic. The great example of the psychoanalysis of an artist is Freud's own essay on Leonardo da Vinci; but this is pretty much an attempt to reconstruct a straight case history. The best example I know of the application of Freudian analysis to literature is in Van Wyck Brooks's book, *The Ordeal of Mark Twain*, in which Brooks uses an incident of Mark Twain's boyhood as a key to his whole career. He has been loudly attacked for this by Bernard de Voto, and he has himself since repudiated the general method on the ground that nobody but an analyst can ever know enough about a writer to make a valid psychoanalytic diagnosis. This is true, of course, and the method has led to bad results where the critic has built a Freudian mechanism out of very slender evidence, and then given us merely a romance based on the supposed working of this mechanism instead of a genuine study of the writer's life and work. But I believe that Brooks had hold of something when he fixed upon that incident of which Mark Twain gave so vivid an account to his biographer—that scene at the deathbed of his father when his mother made him promise that he would not break her heart. If it was not one of those crucial happenings which are supposed to determine the complexes of Freud, it has certainly a typical significance in relation to Mark Twain's whole psychology. The stories that people tell about their childhood are likely to be profoundly symbolic even when they have been partly or wholly made up in the light of later experience. And the attitudes, the compulsions, the emotional "patterns" that recur in the work of a writer are of great interest to the historical critic.

These attitudes and patterns are embedded in the community and the historical moment, and they may indicate its ideals and its diseases as the cell shows the condition of the tissue. The recent scientific experimentation in the combining of Freudian with Marxist method, and of psychoanalysis with anthropology, has had its parallel development in criticism. And there is thus another element added to our equipment for analyzing literary works, and the problem grows still more complex.

The analyst, however, is of course not concerned with the comparative values of his patients any more than the surgeon is. He cannot tell you why the neurotic Dostoevsky produces work of immense value to his fellows, while another man with the same neurotic pattern would become a public menace. Freud himself emphatically states in his study of Leonardo that his method does not make any attempt to account for Leonardo's genius. The problems of comparative value remain after we have investigated the Freudian

psychological factor just as they do after we have given
due attention to the Marxist economic factor and the
racial and geographical factors. No matter how thor-
ough and complete our explanations of works of literature may be from the historical and biographical points
of view, we must be ready to try to estimate the relative
degrees of success attained by the products of the
various periods and the various personalities in some
such way as Eliot and Saintsbury do. We must be able
to tell good from bad, the first-rate from the second-
rate. We shall not otherwise write literary criticism at
all, but merely social or political history as reflected
in literary texts, or psychological case histories from
past eras, or, to take the historical point of view in its
simplest and most academic form, merely chronologies
of books that have been published.

And now how, in these matters of literary art, do we
tell the good art from the bad? Norman Kemp Smith,
the Kantian philosopher, whose courses I was fortunate
enough to take at Princeton twenty-five years ago, used
to tell us that this recognition was based primarily
on an emotional reaction. For purposes of practical
criticism this is a safe assumption to go on. It is possible
to discriminate in a variety of ways the elements that
in any given department go to make a successful work
of literature. Different schools have at different times
demanded different things of literature: *unity, symmetry, universality, originality, vision, inspiration,*

strangeness, suggestiveness, improving morality, socialist realism, etc. But you could have any set of these qualities that any school of writing demanded and still not have a good play, a good novel, a good poem, a good history. If you identify the essence of good literature with any one of these elements or with any combination of them, you simply shift the emotional reaction to the recognition of the elements. Or if you add to your other demands the demand that the writer must have *talent*, you simply shift this recognition to the talent. Once people find some grounds of agreement in the coincidence of their emotional reactions to books, they may be able to discuss these elements profitably; but if they do not have this basic agreement, the discussion will make no sense.

How, you may ask, are we to distinguish this élite who know what they are talking about? They are self-appointed and self-perpetuating, and they will compel you to accept their authority. Impostors may try to put themselves over, but these impostors will not last. The position of the people who understand writing (as is also the case in every other art) is simply that they know what they know, and that they are determined to impose their opinions by main force of eloquence or assertion on the people who do not know.

But what is the *cause* of this emotional reaction which is the critic's divining-rod? This question has

long been an object of study by the branch of philosophy called esthetics, and it has recently been made a
subject of scientific experimentation. Both these kinds
of investigation of literature are likely to be prejudiced
in the eyes of the critic by the fact that they are often
carried on by persons who are themselves obviously
deficient in literary taste. Yet one should not deny the
possible value of explorations in this domain by men of
acute minds who take as their given data the esthetic
emotions of other men.

Almost everybody interested in literature has tried
to explain these emotions to himself; and I of course
have my own explanation.

In my view, all our intellectual activity, in whatever
field it takes place, is an attempt to give a meaning to
our experience—that is, to make life more practicable;
for by understanding things we make it easier to survive
and get around among them. Euclid, working in a
convention of abstractions, shows us relations between
the distances of our unwieldy and cluttered-up environment upon which we are able to count. A drama of
Sophocles also indicates relations between the various
human impulses, which appear so confused and dangerous, and brings out a certain justice of Fate—that is
to say, of the way in which the interaction of these
impulses is seen in the long run to work out—upon
which we can also depend. The kinship from this point
of view of the purposes of science and art appears

particularly clearly with the Greeks, because not only do both Euclid and Sophocles satisfy us by making patterns, but they make very much the same kind of patterns. Euclid's *Elements* takes simple theorems and by a series of logical operations builds them up to a climax in the square on the hypotenuse. A typical drama of Sophocles makes much the same kind of pattern.

Some writers (as well as some scientists) have a more specific message: not content with such an effort as that of Sophocles to make life appear more sensible, and hence to make it more bearable, they try, like Plato, to explain the conditions for making it something different and better. Other kinds of literature, such as Sappho's lyrics, have less philosophical content than Sophocles. A lyric gives us nothing but a pattern imposed on the expression of a feeling; but this pattern of metrical quantities and of balancing consonants and vowels has the effect of reducing the feeling, however unruly or painful it may seem when we experience it in the course of our lives, to something orderly, symmetrical and pleasing. It also relates it to the more comprehensive scheme, works it into the larger texture, of the body of poetic art. The discord has been resolved, the anomaly subjected to discipline. And this control of his emotion by the poet has the effect at second-hand of making it easier for the reader to manage his own emotions. (Why certain sounds and rhythms gratify us more than others and how they are related to the ideas which they are selected as appropriate for conveying, are questions that may be passed on to the scientist.)

And this brings us back to the historical point of view. The experience of mankind is always changing; and the writer who is to be anything more than an echo of his predecessors must always find expression for something which has not yet been expressed, must master new phenomena which have never yet been mastered. With each such victory of the human intellect, whether in the language of philosophy or the language of poetry, we experience a deep satisfaction: we have been cured of some ache of disorder, relieved of some oppressive burden of uncomprehended events.

This relief that brings the sense of power, and with the sense of power, joy, is the emotion which tells us when we are in the presence of a first-rate piece of literature. But, you may at this point object, are not people often solaced and rejoiced by literature of the trashiest kind? They are: crude and limited people do certainly feel such emotions in connection with work that is limited and crude. The man who is more highly organized and has a wider intellectual range will feel it in connection with work that is finer and more complex. The difference between the emotion of the more highly organized man and the emotion of the less highly organized one is merely a matter of gradation. You sometimes encounter books that seem to mark precisely the borderline between work that is definitely superior and work that is definitely bad—the novels of John Steinbeck, for example. When I was speaking a little while back of the experts who establish the standards of taste, I meant the people who can distinguish Grade A and who prefer it to the other grades.

THE ESTHETIC JUDGMENT AND THE ETHICAL JUDGMENT

· By NORMAN FOERSTER ·

The Esthetic Judgment and the
Ethical Judgment

I

WE, it seems, are critical; we are embarrassed with second thoughts; we cannot enjoy anything for hankering to know whereof the pleasure consists; we are lined with eyes; we see with our feet; the time is infected with Hamlet's unhappiness— 'Sicklied o'er with the pale cast of thought.' " These are the words in which Emerson, a hundred years ago, characterized our modern age, an age of criticism.

It is sometimes remarked that there is something wrong with an age which goes in predominantly for criticism. Unhappily there are many other reasons for thinking that there is something wrong with our age. That is precisely why we need criticism. Our modern age, bent upon a return to Nature, has more and more prostituted the humanities—the civilizing forces of religion, philosophy, literature and the arts; and now the totalitarian states, employing with sinister effect the one great creative force of the modern world, science, are intent upon completing the return to Nature, the return to the primitive. These are the times that try men's souls, to see whether we still have souls. These are the times that try men's minds, to see whether we can clarify the phrases we glibly repeat to summon up courage, phrases such as "preserving the values of civilization," "preserving the democratic way of life," "preserving the dignity of man." Without a keener and more earnestly affirmative criticism than we have had, we shall not even know what we wish to preserve, or why it is worth preserving.

Because there is nearly everything wrong with our age, the kind of criticism which can render the greatest service is a general criticism, taking into account the whole of our civilization. Granted that our civilization is highly complex, still we shall have to deal with it in the light of a few simple ideas firmly established. The greater the degree of specialization—the more men are sundered from each other by their preoccupations—to the same extent the need grows for some kind of intellectual and spiritual clearing-house. I refer to the kind of criticism, ranging into diverse fields and vitally connecting them, exemplified in the nineteenth century by Carlyle, Ruskin, Arnold, and Emerson, in the early twentieth century by Chesterton, Babbitt, and More, and in the present day by Jacques Maritain and Lewis Mumford. Such men are not merely critics of literature, they are critics of the foundations of our whole culture.

II

I am to deal in this paper, however, not with general but with literary criticism. What is the task of literary criticism? Let me begin with some negations.

Literary criticism is not concerned with literary works in respect to their *causes*. In our scientific age, it has been customary to think of the intention of a literary work as the sum of many and diverse causes. These causes lie in the author's experience, external and internal, the relation between the world in which he lives, which spreads round him and also back into the past, and his own inner constitution, his developing capacities as man and artist. For each of his works, it is conceived, there is an intricate complex of causes, but we can never be sure that we have found all of them. The study of these causes is a form of history, a blend of literary history, intellectual history, and social history. As scholars know, it is a fascinating study in itself, and it may offer valuable hints to the literary critic, who must use all means to understand the work with which he is dealing. Possibly it is capable of offering more help to the critic than has sometimes been allowed for it by those, including myself, who have reacted against the exaggerated estimate of its services by the sons of Taine; no one, admittedly, has thought through with any finality the relations of the two fields of activity. Clearly, however, the historical study of literature is not literary criticism but at best a preparation for it.

Nor is literary criticism concerned with literary works in respect to their ulterior *effects*. When a work is published—given to the public—it produces (or so the author hopes) some effect upon the public. It may influence the direction of thought or feeling, as in the case of Emerson's *Essays*. It may even lead to more or less change in the realm of practical affairs, ethical, social, political. Thus, *Uncle Tom's Cabin* became one of the causes of the War Between the States, and latterly *The Grapes of Wrath* has begotten a vigorous social response. The high potency of the effects of literary works was a vital concern with Plato, who expelled from his republic all poets except those singing hymns to the gods and praises of famous men, and it is today a vital concern with the dictators of Europe. It has also been a vital concern with American Humanists and Neo-Scholastics, who, since Babbitt's book on *Literature and the American College*, have given fresh life to Matthew Arnold's contention that not science but great literature is the central instrument in the educational process of making men human. And it has been a vital concern with Marxist and other Leftist critics, who realize that literature may become one instrument in the process of making men socialists. Yet it must be admitted that all practical effects, whether good, bad, or indifferent, are extrinsic to the literary work, carrying us away from the work. As causes take us back, effects take us forward. The literary critic must not go either way: he must stay with the work itself: he must deal with its values intrinsically.

Now if there is any sense at all in the history of criticism from Greek antiquity to the present century, two kinds of value are inherent in literature, esthetic and ethical. Let it be granted at once that esthetic value and ethical value are interdependent and, in all strictness, blended inseparably; still, it has not been found possible to discuss them both adequately at one and the same time. Let it be granted also that, logically if not practically, esthetic value must come first, since this determines whether a piece of writing is literature or a piece of non-literary writing.

III

An essential task of the literary critic is to contemplate, analyze, and judge a literary work as a work of art, as a thing of beauty, in its esthetic character. Literature is an art, a form of skill in making, the thing made being a thing of beauty and therefore "a joy forever." The critic is interested, like the artist, in technique, the process of making, but especially he is interested in structure, the esthetic properties of the thing made, its architectonic features such as unity, balance, emphasis, rhythm, and the like, the shapely pattern resulting when all the materials, that is, the emotions, sense perceptions, images, allusions, ideas, ethical insights, have been brought into more or less complete interplay and fullness of tension. When the whole work finally springs to life in his mind, the critic experiences a delight, a joy in the thing of beauty, akin to that of the artist when his vision at length fell into shape. He has a revel similar to that of Mozart, who tells us that musical ideas came streaming to him, began to join one another and kindle his imagination, and formed in his mind into a larger and larger piece till the composition, though unwritten, was complete, and could be seen at a glance. "Then," he said, "I don't hear the notes one after another, as they are hereafter to be played, but it is as if in my fancy they were all at once. And that *is* a revel (*das ist nun ein Schmaus*) ." Inferior works of art do not afford this esthetic experience, and in the greatest art the excitement is imperfect. The critic thus has esthetic exaltations, satisfactions, annoyances, boredoms, which it is his business, as a rational judge, to justify in terms of the esthetic qualities of the works themselves.

I need not say more concerning esthetic judgment; no responsible person questions that it is the business of the literary critic, as of all art critics. A suggestive fact must now be noted: that whereas criticism in the other arts is usually esthetic, criticism in the art of literature is usually not. Why this is I shall inquire presently. Here let me pay tribute to a group of distinguished critics who have so earnestly concentrated upon the esthetic aspect that they have developed a new expertness in the analysis of poetic patterns. Never before, at least in English and American letters, have we had so much close reading, sensitive discrimination, free-ranging alertness expressed in a subtle style suited to the task. I refer, of course, to men like T. S. Eliot, William Empson, John Crowe Ransom, Allen Tate, Cleanth Brooks, and R. P. Blackmur, who, though they have had other interests as well, have excelled in practical criticism of the esthetic aspect of poems. That I am not disposed to underrate their achievement, or the importance of the esthetic point of view, I have perhaps indicated by sponsoring, at the University of Iowa, the recognition of imaginative writing as an art in the graduate school, taking the stand that a play, a novel, a book of verse is as pertinent and honorable in the training of a literary doctor as an academic study in language or literary history or literary criticism.

Having said this, I feel the freer to attack the heresy to which our esthetic critics are inclined, the heresy of the esthetic to which Poe, for example, subscribed. The heresy of the esthetic seems to me as bad as the heresy of the didactic. Both endeavor to make partial truth serve as the whole truth.* Both tend to take us

* Heresies of many sorts have thrived in modern culture because it is so divisive and specialist. The concept of the "economic man," whose activity is independent of moral and political con-

away from literature, the one into problems of morals, the other into problems of esthetics. Indeed, esthetic critics, judging from their line of argument, appear to have scant interest in literature. They begin by speaking of literature; then they turn to the art of literature; then to the art of poetry; then to one kind of poetry, the lyric; and then to one kind of lyric, the metaphysical, in which the poem, as they put it, must not *mean* but *be*, in which substance and form are one, as in the art of music. Now, the view that music, the great modern art, is also the purest art came into vogue with romanticism, along with the corollary view that the essence of literature is lyricism. If music is the purest art, literature is obviously the impurest, so impure that we actually speak of "literature and the arts," as if literature were not an art at all.

But there is another way of ranking the arts, according to their degree of articulateness. From this point of view music is the least and literature the most articulate art. While literature often strives in vain to equal music in wedding form and substance, its special perfection is an articulateness for which the other arts often strive in vain. Whereas music, in the line of

siderations, is but one instance of our tendency to seek purity of thought and achieve unreality. The esthetic man is as artificial as the economic man, as George F. Thomas pointed out in his inaugural lecture at Princeton, "Religion in an Age of Secularism," 1940.

Sidney Lanier, is "Love in search of a word," literature
begins with the word, and builds its structures in terms
of sentences, that is to say, propositions. In literature,
reason and the ethical imagination, contemplating man
and the grounds of his happiness and unhappiness,
speak to us with an incomparable fullness and clarity;
and they do this with maximum facility in the drama,
because the essence of drama, as of human life, is
action, external action in relation to the inner springs
of action. Conceived as the most articulate art, literature has its center, not in the lyric, but rather in the
drama, which lies about midway between works like
The Education of Henry Adams or *The Flowering of
New England*, where literature begins to be differentiated from non-literary prose, and the poems of Vachel
Lindsay or Gertrude Stein, where literature is on the
verge of passing over into music. Or we might reason-
ably say that literature has its center in the narrative
poem or in the novel, since such works as the *Iliad* and
Wilhelm Meister, like *Hamlet* and *Ghosts*, are, whatever their personal content and accent, primarily imaginative representations of life.*

* Works like these, in their rich articulation, would be more
competent than lyrics to enlighten the proverbial Martian as to
the nature of literature and the nature of mundane life. The lyric,
as a fine distillate, a terse comment or gloss upon the text of life,
is capable of an articulateness which is incisive rather than abun-
dant. Its special character is, however, unlimited implication, an
inexhaustible indeterminateness approaching that of music.

IV

We have now come upon the explanation of the fact which I remarked a while ago, that whereas criticism in the other arts is generally esthetic, criticism in the field of literature tends to neglect the esthetic aspect. I deplore the neglect, but the reason for it seems plain enough: that the ethical or philosophic aspect of literature is not only a legitimate but an indispensable concern of the literary critic. I believe that Aristotle was right in thinking of imaginative literature as not only an art giving pleasure or delight, but as a reasonable imitation of life, of human action and human nature; in thinking of imaginative literature as philosophical in a way in which history and science are not. I do not find it necessary to follow Max Eastman and some of his successors in conceiving that all we *know* about life is what science tells us and that the area in which poetry may disport is fast shrinking to nothing. There is, and will always be, not only scientific but human knowledge, the sort of knowledge that we derive from the humanities, notably from literature, knowledge such as we may secure, as Dr. Johnson recognized, by reading Shakespeare, "by reading human sentiments in human language, by scenes from which a hermit may estimate the transactions of the world, and a confessor predict the progress of the passions." Not a little of Johnson's wisdom, which exceeded that of most of our psychologists and sociologists of today, came from great literature.

That poetry contains wisdom was well understood not only by Johnson, but also by Sidney, Dryden, Coleridge, Shelley, Arnold, Emerson, indeed pretty much everybody till we arrive at a few esthetic specialists of the present day. Traditionally they thought of wisdom as instruction, and conceived of the poet as a teacher, an unfortunate terminology because it seems to emphasize the effects of literature, which are the province of the sociological and moral critic. The literary critic is concerned rather with the wisdom *inherent* in literature, with the judgment of its ethical soundness, the firmness and range of its imitation of life. He repeats the Horatian formula not because it is traditional but because its soundness has made it traditional, saying with Robert Frost, the wisest of our contemporary poets, that a poem "begins in delight and ends in wisdom," or with Paul Engle that a poem affords a "wise excitement" or "intense wisdom." He is content to say, if you insist, that delight is all, but in that case he will add at once that the delight comes from the wisdom expressed as well as from the expression of the wisdom.

If, then, literary criticism is an esthetic judgment, it is equally an ethical judgment, and both judgments are needed to determine the "greatness" of literary works. A poem like "A Psalm of Life" falls short on both counts: it is bungling in its art, stereotyped in its wisdom. A poem like "Tintern Abbey" is great esthetically; as we have come increasingly to see, it is ethically vital but unsound; in sum, this poem is a superb expression of unwisdom. On the other hand, the poem which Wordsworth addressed to Milton (along with some of his other sonnets deeply inspired by the nobility of the English tradition) has greatness on the two counts, is both finely formed and wisely conceived.

To estimate the greatness of literary works, which is the main business of literary criticism, what is needed is a rounded estimate, esthetic and ethical. In a truly rounded estimate, the two tasks will be inseparable, will interpenetrate as intimately as in the organic unity of the literary work itself. But in fact such an organic criticism is impossible, and indeed all interpretation and evaluation is, strictly speaking, inept. Change the words and you change the thought. Paraphrase and you rob the text of much of its meaning. Translate and you impoverish or else create a new thing. Say anything whatever about a piece of literature in either its esthetic or its ethical aspect and you dilute or denature what is there. The only completely scrupulous critic is, therefore, the completely silent critic. Since this asceticism is more than critic flesh can endure, critics may be permitted to go on criticizing as well as they can, turning, again and again, consciously or not, from one kind of judgment to the other, violating the simultaneity of literature by resorting to alternation. Or they may be permitted to let one kind of judgment preponderate, because it is the kind in which they are interested or gifted, provided that they leave room, in their total theory, for others to practise more fully the other kind of judgment. Unfortunately some critics will be tempted to go farther, to become exclusive and intolerant, to employ one of the two judgments and decry the other. Preoccupied with a half-truth, such critics will fall into the heresy of estheticism or the heresy of didacticism.*

V

The theory of literary criticism I have sketched is that of the so-called Neo-Humanists. Why have they so inadequately practised it? Why has their interest in the esthetic properties of literature always been so definitely secondary, their interest in its ethical properties so definitely primary? Why did Babbitt and More, the leaders of the group, display an increasing aloofness

---

* From the Greeks till the late nineteenth century, the greater peril was didacticism; since the *Décadents* it has been estheticism.

Treating the ethical quality of the artifact as but one element in a system of relationships on a par with such other elements as rhythm, imagery, and diction, an accomplished group of critics today has tended to a confined and unwholesome estheticism which contrasts with the wide and free humanity of literature itself. As I. A. Richards suggests, many naturally superior critical minds, reacting against the "wild asses" who crudely applied the criterion of moral effect, "have virtually shut themselves up in a paddock."

even from literature? Why did the author of so many
accomplished literary studies in the Shelburne series
select as his crowning achievement a profound study
of the Christian religion? And why did Babbitt, one of
whose first books was on the modern confusion of the
arts, attain his most substantial achievement in a book
on democracy and close his career with a book on Hindu
religion?

I have already answered these questions by saying
that More and Babbitt were general critics. They were
convinced that there is nearly everything wrong with
modern civilization. Living in a time of complacent
naturalism, when the idea of progress promised a
Utopia, and science a method for attaining it, they
made themselves unpopular by asserting that such a de-
luded program could only lead to the destruction of
our civilization. To others, such as the socialists, who
saw something fundamentally wrong in our civilization but who sought a remedy in a new economic system, they replied that the higher issues must be faced
before the lower, since "the economic problem will be
found to run into the political problem, and the political problem in turn into the philosophical problem, and
the philosophical problem itself to be almost indis-
solubly bound up at last with the religious problem."
Believing that our civilization had gone wrong on first
principles, they were not content to be literary critics;
they were general critics, and finally religious critics.

That it is possible to serve the same high ends without leaving the field of literary criticism has been shown most clearly, perhaps, by a scholar deeply influenced by them, G. R. Elliott of Amherst College. His *Cycle of Modern Poetry*, published in that year of economic hubris and nemesis, 1929, is not a work of philosophy, nor a work in which literature is merely used as material for philosophic purposes; it is a genuine piece of literary criticism, in which a sensitive esthetic discrimination interplays with keen ethical insight. With this double awareness Mr. Elliott considers the whole cycle of English poetry since the eighteenth century, beginning with Shelley and Byron, ending with Hardy, Frost, and their immediate successors. This great poetic impulse, as he conceives, is "now pretty well exhausted": "Poetry today, in England and America, is groping for a fresh direction." Mr. Elliott's prevailing theme is the subjection of modern poetry; his purpose, to show how it may attain freedom. "Perhaps never before," he says, "has poetry been so widely eager and experimental and, at the same time, so shortly tethered." He finds it tethered on one side to art because of a mistaken notion of the relation of poetry to art, and on the other side to something which is lacking large human meanings. His conclusion is that our poetry can rewin its freedom only by traversing anew "the great zones of the religious and moral imagination" with the aid of Milton "as a living classic and as our chief guide." A serious effort at poetic freedom will compel us to transcend modern ideas of human freedom. To illustrate, Mr. Elliott contrasts Whitman's declaration at the close of the Civil War: "Be not disheartened, affection shall solve the problems of freedom yet," with what Milton wrote at the close of the English Civil War: "Instead of fretting with vexation, or thinking that you can lay the blame on anyone but yourselves, know that to be free is the same thing as to be pious, to be wise, to be temperate and just, to be frugal and abstinent, and lastly, to be magnanimous and brave." Whitman's sentence, Mr. Elliott comments, "is the theme of nineteenth century poetry: its social unreality is now glaring; it is a worn-out imagining." But the passage from Milton "speaks to us, in our post-war era, like the voice of destiny close to our ear."

There may be many reasons, as the general critic could point out, why we need to deepen our notion of freedom, but Mr. Elliott, as literary critic, is concerned with one reason only: to restore the health of modern poetry. He wishes to free poetry from its deforming aberrations by returning it to the great tradition. Once reconnected with a truly usable past, it will have some chance to move forward to a central creativeness, instead of deploying barrenly in technical experiment.

To become great once more, poetry needs a humane philosophy.*

VI

Now, the prominence given by humanist critics—even by Mr. Elliott—to the philosophical aspect of literature has been frequently condemned, sometimes by those who happen to prefer a different philosophy, sometimes by those who assert that the literary critic has no business trafficking with philosophy at all. I wish to answer the latter charge.

The answer lies, I think, in a distinction between systematic and literary philosophy. By systematic philosophy I mean, of course, the kind of philosophy which is outlined in the histories of philosophy, the kind with which university departments of philosophy busy themselves. With philosophy in this sense the literary critic should seek friendship but not wedlock. In the equipment of a critic, as W. C. Brownell put it, "a tincture at least of philosophic training may be timidly prescribed. . . . Drenched in philosophy, the critical faculty is almost certain to drown." Perhaps it

---

* In the decade since *The Cycle of Modern Poetry* appeared, efforts have been extended to find a usable past in the poetry of Milton's century, especially in that of Donne, but with emphasis on a shift in technique rather than on a return to a humane philosophy.

Literature needs also, as Mr. Elliott is well aware, a humane society, a usable present, since writers absorb their age into their lives and work and are nourished by it.

would be better to say that the more philosophy a critic can carry without altering his center of gravity, the sharper his criticism will be in its logical niceties, the tighter and richer in its intellectual texture. An excess of philosophy, however, may easily betray him into a rigid application of ideas to a field which is, after all, not amenable to philosophic standards. This is why the professional philosopher is so rarely a good literary critic. He is simply not at home. Despite all his training in thought, he is likely to manhandle thought in literary works. He is handicapped not merely because of his ineptness in the realm of the concrete and sensuous, but, far more seriously, because of his inclination to want a writer to look as firmly philosophic as possible and then to belabor him when he is literary, that is to say the greater part of the time. It is the very nature of literary philosophy to be loose, to be unsystematic, to be open not closed, to be generous not exclusive, to be suggestive not decisive. While the most articulate of the arts, literature does not aim at the specialized articulation of philosophy, the perfect web of abstract thought. Writers, like people in general, have a philosophy of life, not a formulated scheme such as professional philosophers require. The informal philosophies of our writers can be appropriately judged only by literary critics, who, being literary, share the writers' distrust of fixed systems, the writers' assumption that reason cannot exhaust the whole of reality, the conviction of a man like Plato, who was man of letters as well as philosopher, that logical explication must give way to symbol and myth when the highest truths are to be adumbrated.

Literature is not philosophy; it is, if I may quote what I have said elsewhere, "the record, in terms of beauty, of the striving of Mankind to know and express itself." Blending its love of beauty with its love of truth, it aims at nothing more than a working philosophy, enough articulation to give it firmness. Its subject is, essentially, the inner nature of man; it offers a working philosophy of man, or that "philosophy of wisdom" of which Erasmus spoke. It is not a parasitic but an independent growth. It may feed upon the works of systematic thinkers, but somewhat casually, not strictly following their logic. It could, in fact, get along without them, for literature has its own philosophic life and would go on even if philosophy had never been or should cease to be. Writers are thinkers, unsystematic thinkers, for whom everything is grist: experience here and now, the traditions of literature and the arts, history, science, religion, philosophy, all the concerns of man.

This is equally true of literary critics. Their activity is that of the writers; they too achieve some sort of working philosophy, but with them the end aimed at is different since they are not makers but judges. For them a working philosophy is requisite, not for inform-

ing works of art with significance, but for evaluating the
significance of works of art. And in order to evaluate,
they must be a great deal more conscious of their working philosophy than the artist. To the artist a philosophy is ideally an ardent faith, something so profoundly
felt that it no longer needs reflection, something given
which only asks to be formed or made, so that he is
free to bestow upon it his full attention as an artist.
Sound, therefore, is the advice which Jacques Maritain
addresses to the artist: "Do not *separate* your art from
your faith. But leave *distinct* what is distinct. Do not try
to blend by force what life unites so well. If you were
to make your esthetic an article of faith, you would
spoil your faith. If you were to make your devotion a
rule of artistic operation, or turn the desire to edify
into a method of your art, you would spoil your art."
But this unanalyzed integrity which M. Maritain
recommends to the artist is not for the critic as well.
His task is not to shape a symbol but to separate elements, to distinguish, to explain, to classify, to compare and contrast, to weigh, to reach a palpable conclusion, and for this rational task he needs a rational
control of his philosophy.

There are those, to be sure, who would have the literary critic set aside his philosophy if it happens to
be different from that of the work he is criticizing. They
would have him suppress his disbelief. For the time
being he should be like a guileless child, willing to

credit the fairy tale. This I think is often impossible, and in any case absurd. But not wholly absurd. Let me explain by describing how, it seems to me, a good critic will read a book new to him. He will read it in two ways, first one way and then the other, or else in the two ways simultaneously. One way we may speak of as "feeling the book," the other as "thinking the book." By feeling the book I mean passively responding to the will of the author, securing the total impression aimed at. If the book accords with the critic's tastes and beliefs, this will be easy; otherwise, he will have to attempt an abeyance of disbelief, a full acceptance of the work for the time being, in order to understand it. But understanding is not criticism, and therefore he must read it another way, "thinking the book," that is, analyzing closely the esthetic pattern and the ethical burden, and reflecting upon these in terms of his criteria until he is ready with a mature opinion of the book's value. If obliged to suspend disbelief when reading the first way, he is now obliged to state and justify his disbelief.

A good critic will read in this double fashion, I think, no matter what his working philosophy may be. How much of extant literature a critic can genuinely accept and admire will depend on his particular philosophy. To the thoroughgoing naturalist of the present day, the great bulk of literature from Homer to the middle nineteenth century is, on the ethical side, misguided, dated, of antiquarian interest. To the humanist, on the other hand, this same body of literature represents, on the ethical side, the "wisdom of the ages" as opposed to the brief unwisdom of the romantics and the naturalists. Since the romantics pretended to high wisdom and the naturalists have proclaimed their austere love of truth, the humanist deems it appropriate to meet them on their own ground and to try to demonstrate their philosophic immaturity. Today, when a crude naturalism runs rampant in literature and the arts, as well as in the realm of political thought and action, the humanist conceives that he may be forgiven his comparative indifference to the esthetic aspects of contemporary writings, may be permitted to dwell upon the subversiveness of their ethical significance, their celebration of the indignity of man, their basic defeatism.

How much of the dignity of man of which we prate is symbolized in our literature, the true mirror of our thoughts? Sometimes it is travestied by the lingering formulas of romanticism, more often it is drably belied by books and plays in which man is pictured as irrational and unfree, in ugly bondage to heredity and environment. To the pale cast of our thought, what a piece of nature is a man! How ignoble in rationalizing! How infinite in blundering! Here is something to which the literary critic may well apply a humane philosophy, bringing his literary judgment into relation with a general or final judgment, if he would not be numbered among those "Irresponsibles" whom Archibald Mac-Leish has excoriated.

If the life of man is indeed as nasty and brutish as the most typical literature of our time represents it, the victory of the organized, mechanized evil which is now loose in the world will only confirm a disaster that has already taken place. As Walter Lippmann declared with unwonted fervor in an address to his Harvard Class, what has made possible the victories of this scientized evil is "the lazy, self-indulgent materialism, the amiable, lackadaisical, footless, confused complacency of the free nations of the world. They have dissipated, like wastrels and drunkards, the inheritance of freedom and order that came to them from hardworking, thrifty, faithful, believing, and brave men. The disaster in the midst of which we are living is a disaster in the character of men."

I think that Mr. Lippmann is right. Vast armaments alone will not save us. We must also rewin our all but lost inheritance of freedom and order, and with freedom and order that on which they depend, belief in the dignity of man. And this in turn can come only through a religious renewal of belief in man as a spiritual being, or if that is beyond our attainment, a humanistic renewal of belief in man as a rational and free animal, a belief still richly current in the time of Washington and Jefferson, a belief that comes down to us all the way from ancient Greece. We have had our "return to

Nature"; it is time for another great historical return, the "return to Man."

If the literary critic has no concern with such problems, he might as well close up shop and let the tempest ride.

CRITICISM AS PURE SPECULATION

· By JOHN CROWE RANSOM ·

Criticism as Pure Speculation

I

I WILL testify to the weight of responsibility felt by the critic who enters a serial discussion with such other lecturers as Mr. Wilson, Mr. Auden, and Mr. Foerster; and delivers his opinion to an audience at Princeton, where live at least two eminent critics, in Mr. Tate and Mr. Blackmur, and one eminent esthetician, in Mr. Greene.

Indeed, Mr. Blackmur and Mr. Greene have recently published books* which bear on this discussion. Mr. Blackmur's essays are probably all that can be expected of a critic who has not explicitly submitted them to the discipline of general esthetics; but with that limitation the best critic in the world might expose himself to review and reproach. Mr. Greene's esthetic studies, in turn, may have wonderful cogency as philosophical discourse; but if throughout them he should fail to maintain intimate contact with the actual works of art he would invite damaging attentions from the literary critics. I am far from suggesting such proceedings against them. Mr. Blackmur has his native phil-

* *The Expense of Greatness*, by R. P. Blackmur, Arrow Editions, 1940; *The Arts and the Art of Criticism*, by Theodore Meyer Greene, Princeton University Press, 1940.

[91]

osophical sense to keep his critical foundations from sliding into the sea. Mr. Greene is in a very strong position: recognizing the usual weakness of formal esthetics, he tries a device to secure his own studies against it; for when he needs them he uses reports from reputable actual critics upon the practices in the several arts. A chasm, perhaps an abyss, separates the critic and the esthetician ordinarily, if the books in the library are evidence. But the authority of criticism depends on its coming to terms with esthetics, and the authority of literary esthetics depends on its coming to terms with criticism. Mr. Greene is an esthetician, and his department is philosophy, but he has subscribed in effect to this thesis. I am a sort of critic, and my department is English poetry, so that I am very much in Mr. Blackmur's position; and I subscribe to the thesis, and am altogether disposed to solicit Mr. Greene's philosophical services.

When we inquire into the "intent of the critic," we mean: the intent of the generalized critic, or critic as such. We will concede that any professional critic is familiar with the technical practices of poets so long as these are conventional, and is expert in judging when they perform them brilliantly, and when only fairly, or badly. We expect a critical discourse to cover that much, but we know that more is required. The most famous poets of our own time, for example, make wide departures from conventional practices: how are they to be judged? Innovations in poetry, or even conventions when pressed to their logical limits, cause the ordinary critic to despair. They cause the good critic to review his esthetic principles; perhaps to re-formulate his esthetic principles. He tries the poem against his best philosophical conception of the peculiar character that a poem should have.

Mr. T. S. Eliot is an extraordinarily sensitive critic. But when he discusses the so-called "metaphysical" poetry, he surprises us by refusing to study the so-called "conceit" which is its reputed basis; he observes instead that the metaphysical poets of the seventeenth century are more like their immediate predecessors than the latter are like the eighteenth and nineteenth century poets, and then he goes into a very broad philosophical comparison between two whole "periods" or types of poetry. I think it has come to be understood that his comparison is unsound; it has not proved workable enough to assist critics who have otherwise borrowed liberally from his critical principles. (It contains the famous dictum about the "sensibility" of the earlier poets, it imputes to them a remarkable ability to "feel their thought," and to have a kind of "experience" in which the feeling cannot be differentiated from the thinking.) Now there is scarcely another critic equal to Eliot at distinguishing the practices of two poets who are closely related. He is supreme as a comparative critic when the relation in question is delicate and subtle; that is, when it is a matter of close perception and not a radical difference in kind. But this line of criticism never goes far enough. In Eliot's own range of criticism the line does not always answer. He is forced by discontinuities in the poetic tradition into sweeping theories that have to do with esthetics, the philosophy of poetry; and his own philosophy probably seems to us insufficient, the philosophy of the literary man.

The intent of the critic may well be, then, first to read his poem sensitively, and make comparative judgments about its technical practice, or, as we might say, to emulate Eliot. Beyond that, it is to read and remark the poem knowingly; that is, with an esthetician's understanding of what a poem generically "is."

Before I venture, with inadequate argument, to describe what I take to be the correct understanding of poetry, I would like to describe two other understandings which, though widely professed, seem to me misunderstandings. First, there is a smart and bellettristic theory of poetry which may be called "psychologistic." Then there is an altogether staid and commonplace theory which is moralistic. Of these in their order.

II

It could easily be argued about either of these untenable conceptions of poetry that it is an act of despair to which critics resort who cannot find for the discourse of poetry any precise differentia to remove it from the category of science. Psychologistic critics hold that poetry is addressed primarily to the feelings and motor impulses; they remind us frequently of its contrast with the coldness, the unemotionality, of science, which is supposed to address itself to the pure cognitive mind. Mr. Richards came out spectacularly for the doctrine, and furnished it with detail of the greatest ingenuity. He very nearly severed the dependence of poetic effect upon any standard of objective knowledge or belief. But the feelings and impulses which he represented as gratified by the poem were too tiny and numerous to be named. He never identified them; they seemed not so much psychological as infra-psychological. His was an esoteric poetic: it could not be disproved. But neither could it be proved, and I think it is safe at this distance to say that eventually his readers, and Richards himself, lost interest in it as being an improvisation, much too unrelated to the public sense of a poetic experience.

With other critics psychologism of some sort is an old story, and one that will probably never cease to be told. For, now that all of us know about psychology, there must always be persons on hand precisely conditioned to declare that poetry is an emotional discourse indulged in resentment and compensation for science, the bleak cognitive discourse in its purity. It becomes less a form of knowledge than a form of "expression." The critics are willing to surrender the honor of objectivity to science if they may have the luxury of subjectivity for poetry. Science will scarcely object. But one or two things have to be said about that. In every experience, even in science, there is feeling. No discourse can sustain itself without interest, which is feeling. The interest, or the feeling, is like an automatic index to the human value of the proceeding—which would not otherwise proceed. Mr. Eliseo Vivas is an esthetician who might be thought to reside in the camp of the enemy, for his affiliations are positivist; yet in a recent essay he writes about the "passion" which sustains the heroic labors of the scientist as one bigger and more intense than is given to most men.

I do not mean to differ with that judgment at all in remarking that we might very well let the passions and the feelings take care of themselves; it is precisely what we do in our pursuit of science. The thing to attend to is the object to which they attach. As between two similar musical phrases, or between two similar lines of poetry, we may often defy the most proficient psychologist to distinguish the one feeling-response from the other; unless we permit him to say at long last that one is the kind of response that would be made to the first line, and the other is the kind of response that would be made to the second line. But that is to do, after much wasted motion, what I have just suggested: to attend to the poetic object and let the feelings take care of themselves. It is their business to "respond." There may be a feeling correlative with the minutest alteration in an object, and adequate to it, but we shall hardly know. What we do know is that the feelings are grossly inarticulate if we try to abstract them and take their testimony in their own language. Since it is not the intent of the critic to be inarticulate, his discriminations must be among the objects. We understand this so well intuitively that the critic seems to us in possession of some esoteric knowledge, some magical insight, if he appears to be intelligent elsewhere and yet refers confidently to the "tone" or "quality" or "value" of the feeling he discovers in a given line. Probably he is bluffing. The distinctness resides in the cognitive or "semantical" objects denoted by the words. When Richards bewilders us by reporting affective and motor disturbances that are too tiny for definition, and other critics by reporting disturbances that are too massive and gross, we cannot fail to grow suspicious of this whole way of insight as incompetent.

Eliot has a special version of psychologistic theory which looks extremely fertile, though it is broad and nebulous as his psychologistic terms require it to be. He likes to regard the poem as a structure of emotion and feeling. But the emotion is singular, there being only one emotion per poem, or at least per passage: it is the central emotion or big emotion which attaches to the main theme or situation. The feeling is plural. The emotion combines with many feelings; these are our little responses to the single words and phrases, and he does not think of them as being parts of the central emotion or even related to it. The terminology is greatly at fault, or we should recognize at once, I think, a principle that might prove very valuable. I would not answer for the conduct of a technical philosopher in assessing this theory; he might throw it away, out of patience with its jargon. But a lay philosopher who respects his Eliot and reads with all his sympathy might salvage a good thing from it, though I have not heard of anyone doing so. He would try to escape from the affective terms, and translate Eliot into more intelligible language. Eliot would be saying in effect that a poem has a central logic or situation or "paraphrasable core" to which an appropriate interest doubtless attaches, and that in this respect the poem is like a discourse of science behind which lies the sufficient passion. But he would be saying at the same time, and this is the important thing, that the poem has also a context of lively local details to which other and independent interests attach; and that in this respect it is unlike the discourse of science. For the detail of scientific discourse intends never to be independent of the thesis (either objectively or affectively) but always functional, and subordinate to the realization of the thesis. To say that is to approach to a structural understanding of poetry, and to the kind of understanding that I wish presently to urge.

III

As for the moralistic understanding of poetry, it is sometimes the specific moralists, men with moral axes to grind, and incidentally men of unassailable public position, who cherish that; they have a "use" for poetry. But not exclusively, for we may find it held also by critics who are more spontaneous and innocent: apparently they fall back upon it because it attributes some special character to poetry, which otherwise refuses to yield up to them a character. The moral interest is so much more frequent in poetry than in science that they decide to offer its moralism as a differentia.

This conception of poetry is of the greatest antiquity —it antedates the evolution of close esthetic philosophy, and persists beside it too. Plato sometimes spoke of poetry in this light—perhaps because it was recommended to him in this light—but nearly always scornfully. In the *Gorgias*, and other dialogues, he represents the poets as moralizing, and that is only what he, in the person of Socrates, is doing at the very moment, and given to doing; but he considers the moralizing of poets as mere "rhetoric," or popular philosophy, and unworthy of the accomplished moralist who is the real or technical philosopher. Plato understood very well

[99]

that the poet does not conduct a technical or an original discourse like that of the scientist—and the term includes here the moral philosopher—and that close and effective moralizing is scarcely to be had from him. It is not within the poet's power to offer that if his intention is to offer poetry; for the poetry and the morality are so far from being identical that they interfere a little with each other.

Few famous estheticians in the history of philosophy have cared to bother with the moralistic conception; many critics have, in all periods. Just now we have at least two schools of moralistic critics contending for the official possession of poetry. One is the Neo-Humanist, and Mr. Foerster has identified himself with that. The other is the Marxist, and I believe it is represented in some degree and shade by Mr. Wilson, possibly by Mr. Auden. I have myself taken profit from the discussions by both schools, but recently I have taken more—I suppose this is because I was brought up in a scholastic discipline rather like the Neo-Humanist—from the writings of the Marxist critics. One of the differences is that the Neo-Humanists believe in the "respectable" virtues, but the Marxists believe that respectability is the greatest of vices, and equate respectable with "genteel." That is a very striking difference, and I think it is also profound.

But I do not wish to be impertinent; I can respect both these moralities, and appropriate moral values from both. The thing I wish to argue is not the comparative merits of the different moralities by which poetry is judged, but their equal inadequacy to the reading of the poet's intention. The moralistic critics wish to isolate and discuss the "ideology" or theme or paraphrase of the poem and not the poem itself. But even to the practitioners themselves, if they are sophisticated, comes sometimes the apprehension that this is moral rather than literary criticism. I have not seen the papers of my colleagues in this discussion, for that was against the rules, but it is reported to me that both Mr. Wilson and Mr. Foerster concede in explicit words that criticism has both the moral and the esthetic branches; Mr. Wilson may call them the "social" and esthetic branches. And they would hold the critical profession responsible for both branches. Under these circumstances the critics cease to be mere moralists and become dualists; that is better. My feeling about such a position would be that the moral criticism we shall have with us always, and have had always, and that it is easy—comparatively speaking—and that what is hard, and needed, and indeed more and more urgent after all the failures of poetic understanding, is a better esthetic criticism. This is the branch which is all but invariably neglected by the wise but morally zealous critics; they tend to forget their dual responsibility. I think I should go so far as to think that, in strictness, the business of the literary critic is exclusively with an esthetic criticism. The business of the moralist will naturally, and properly, be with something else.

If we have the patience to read for a little while in the anthology, paying some respect to the varieties of substance actually in the poems, we cannot logically attribute ethical character by definition to poetry; for that character is not universal in the poems. And if we have any faith in a community of character among the several arts, we are stopped quickly from risking such a definition for art at large. To claim a moral content for most of sculpture, painting, music, or architecture, is to plan something dialectically very roundabout and subtle, or else to be so arbitrary as to invite instant exposure. I should think the former alternative is impractical, and the latter, if it is not stupid, is masochistic.

The moralistic critics are likely to retort upon their accusers by accusing them in turn of the vapid doc-trine known as Art for Art's Sake. And with frequent justice; but again we are likely to receive the impression that it is just because Art for Art's Sake, the historic doctrine, proved empty, and availed them so little esthetically, like all the other doctrines that came into default, that they have fled to their moralism. Moral-ism does at least impute to poetry a positive substance, as Art for Art's Sake does not. It asserts an autonomy for art, which is excellent; but autonomy to do what? Only to be itself, and to reduce its interpreters to a

tautology? With its English adherents in the 'nineties
the doctrine seemed to make only a negative requirement of art, that is, that it should be anti-Victorian as
we should say today, a little bit naughty and immoral
perhaps, otherwise at least non-moral, or carefully
squeezed dry of moral substance. An excellent example
of how two doctrines, inadequate equally but in oppo-
site senses, may keep themselves alive by abhorring
each other's errors.

It is highly probable that the poem considers an
ethical situation, and there is no reason why it should
repel this from its consideration. But, if I may say so
without being accused of verbal trifling, the poetic
consideration of the ethical situation is not the same as
the ethical consideration of it. The straight ethical
consideration would be prose; it would be an act of
interested science, or an act of practical will. The poetic
consideration, according to Schopenhauer, is the objectification of this act of will; that is, it is our contem-
plation and not our exercise of will, and therefore
qualitatively a very different experience; knowledge
without desire. That doctrine also seems too negative
and indeterminate. I will put the point as I see it in
another way. It should be a comfort to the moralist
that there is ordinarily a moral composure in the poem,
as if the poet had long known good and evil, and made
his moral choice between them once and for all. Art is
post-ethical rather than unethical. In the poem there is

an increment of meaning which is neither the ethical content nor opposed to the ethical content. The poetic experience would have to stop for the poet who is developing it, or for the reader who is following it, if the situation which is being poetically treated should turn back into a situation to be morally determined; if, for example, the situation were not a familiar one, and one to which we had habituated our moral wills; for it would rouse the moral will again to action, and make the poetic treatment impossible under its heat. Art is more cool than hot, and a moral fervor is as disastrous to it as a burst of passion itself. We have seen Marxists recently so revolted by Shakespeare's addiction to royal or noble *personae* that they cannot obtain esthetic experience from the plays; all they get is moral agitation. In another art, we know, and doubtless we approve, the scruple of the college authorities in not permitting the "department of fine arts" to direct the collegians in painting in the nude. Doctor Hanns Sachs, successor to Freud, in a recent number of his *American Imago*, gives a story from a French author as follows:

"He tells that one evening strolling along the streets of Paris he noticed a row of slot machines which for a small coin showed pictures of women in full or partial undress. He observed the leering interest with which men of all kind and description, well dressed and shabby, boys and old men, enjoyed the peep show. He remarked that they all avoided one of these machines, and wondering what uninteresting pictures it might show, he put his penny in the slot. To his great astonishment the generally shunned picture turned out to be the Venus of Medici. Now he begins to ponder: Why does nobody get excited about her? She is decidedly feminine and not less naked than the others which hold such strong fascination for everybody. Finally he finds a satisfactory answer: They fight shy of her because she is beautiful."

And Doctor Sachs, though in his own variety of jargon, makes a number of wise observations about the psychic conditions precedent to the difficult apprehension of beauty. The experience called beauty is beyond the powerful ethical will precisely as it is beyond the animal passion, and indeed these last two are competitive, and coordinate. Under the urgency of either we are incapable of appreciating the statue or understanding the poem.

IV

The ostensible substance of the poem may be anything at all which words may signify: an ethical situation, a passion, a train of thought, a flower or landscape, a thing. This substance receives its poetic increment. It might be safer to say it receives some subtle and mysterious alteration under poetic treatment, but I

will risk the cruder formula: the ostensible substance
is increased by an x, which is an increment. The poem
actually continues to contain its ostensible substance,
which is not fatally diminished from its prose state: that
is its logical core, or paraphrase. The rest of the poem is
x, which we are to find.

We feel the working of this simple formula when we
approach a poetry with our strictest logic, provided we
can find deliverance from certain inhibiting philosophical prepossessions into which we have been conditioned by the critics we have had to read. Here is Lady
Macbeth planning a murder with her husband:

> When Duncan is asleep—
> Whereto the rather shall his hard day's journey
> Soundly invite him—his two chamberlains
> Will I with wine and wassail so convince,
> That memory, the warder of the brain,
> Shall be a fume, and the receipt of reason
> A limbec only; when in swinish sleep
> Their drenched natures lie as in a death,
> What cannot you and I perform upon
> The unguarded Duncan? what not put upon
> His spongy officers, who shall bear the guilt
> Of our great quell?

It is easy to produce the prose argument or paraphrase
of this speech; it has one upon which we shall all agree.
But the passage is more than its argument. Any detail,

with this speaker, seems capable of being expanded in some direction which is not that of the argument. For example, Lady Macbeth says she will make the chamberlains drunk so that they will not remember their charge, nor keep their wits about them. But it is indifferent to this argument whether memory according to the old psychology is located at the gateway to the brain, whether it is to be disintegrated into fume as of alcohol, and whether the whole receptacle of the mind is to be turned into a still. These are additions to the argument both energetic and irrelevant—though they do not quite stop or obscure the argument. From the point of view of the philosopher they are excursions into particularity. They give, in spite of the argument, which would seem to be perfectly self-sufficient, a sense of the real density and contingency of the world in which arguments and plans have to be pursued. They bring out the private character which the items of an argument can really assume if we look at them. This character spreads out in planes at right angles to the course of the argument, and in effect gives to the discourse another dimension, not present in a perfectly logical prose. We are expected to have sufficient judgment not to let this local character take us too far or keep us too long from the argument.

All this would seem commonplace remark, I am convinced, but for those philosophically timid critics who are afraid to think that the poetic increment is local and irrelevant, and that poetry cannot achieve its own virtue and keep undiminished the virtues of prose at the same time. But I will go a little further in the hope of removing the sense of strangeness in the analysis. I will offer a figurative definition of a poem.

A poem is, so to speak, a democratic state, whereas a prose discourse—mathematical, scientific, ethical, or practical and vernacular—is a totalitarian state. The intention of a democratic state is to perform the work of state as effectively as it can perform it, subject to one reservation of conscience: that it will not despoil its members, the citizens, of the free exercise of their own private and independent characters. But the totalitarian state is interested solely in being effective, and regards the citizens as no citizens at all; that is, regards them as functional members whose existence is totally defined by their allotted contributions to its ends; it has no use for their private characters, and therefore no provision for them. I indicate of course the extreme or polar opposition between two polities, without denying that a polity may come to us rather mixed up.

In this trope the operation of the state as a whole represents of course the logical paraphrase or argument of the poem. The private character of the citizens represents the particularity asserted by the parts in the poem. And this last is our x.

For many years I had seen—as what serious observer has not—that a poem as a discourse differentiated itself from prose by its particularity, yet not to the point of sacrificing its logical cogency or universality. But I could get no further. I could not see how real particularity could get into a universal. The object of esthetic studies became for me a kind of discourse, or a kind of natural configuration, which like any other discourse or configuration claimed universality, but which consisted actually, and notoriously, of particularity. The poem was concrete, yet universal, and in spite of Hegel I could not see how the two properties could be identified as forming in a single unit the "concrete universal." It is usual, I believe, for persons at this stage to assert that somehow the apparent diffuseness or particularity in the poem gets itself taken up or "assimilated" into the logic, to produce a marvellous kind of unity called a "higher unity," to which ordinary discourse is not eligible. The belief is that the "idea" or theme proves itself in poetry to be even more dominating than in prose by overcoming much more energetic resistance than usual on the part of the materials, and the resistance, as attested in the local development of detail, is therefore set not to the debit but to the credit of the unifying power of the poetic spirit. A unity of that kind is one which philosophers less audacious and more factual than Hegel would be loath to claim. Critics incline to call it, rather esoterically, an "imaginative" rather than a logical unity, but one supposes they mean a mystical, an ineffable, unity. I for one could neither grasp it nor deny it. I believe that is not an uncommon situation for poetic analysts to find themselves in.

It occurred to me at last that the solution might be very easy if looked for without what the positivists call "metaphysical prepossessions." Suppose the logical substance remained there all the time, and was in no way specially remarkable, while the particularity came in by accretion, so that the poem turned out partly universal, and partly particular, but with respect to different parts. I began to remark the dimensions of a poem, or other work of art. The poem was not a mere moment in time, nor a mere point in space. It was sizeable, like a house. Apparently it had a "plan," or a central frame of logic, but it had also a huge wealth of local detail, which sometimes fitted the plan functionally or served it, and sometimes only subsisted comfortably under it; in either case the house stood up. But it was the political way of thinking which gave me the first analogy which seemed valid. The poem was like a democratic state, in action, and observed both macroscopically and microscopically.

The house occurred also, and provided what seems to be a more negotiable trope under which to construe the poem. A poem is a *logical structure* having a *local texture*. These terms have been actually though not systematically employed in literary criticism. To my imagination they are architectural. The walls of my room are obviously structural; the beams and boards have a function; so does the plaster, which is the visible aspect of the final wall. The plaster might have remained naked, aspiring to no character, and purely functional. But actually it has been painted, receiving color; or it has been papered, receiving color and design, though these have no structural value; and perhaps it has been hung with tapestry, or with paintings, for "decoration." The paint, the paper, the tapestry are texture. It is logically unrelated to structure. But I indicate only a few of the textural possibilities in architecture. There are not fewer of them in poetry.

The intent of the good critic becomes therefore to examine and define the poem with respect to its structure and its texture. If he has nothing to say about its texture he has nothing to say about it specifically as a poem, but is treating it only insofar as it is prose.

I do not mean to say that the good critic will necessarily employ my terms.

V

Many critics today are writing analytically and with close intelligence, in whatever terms, about the logical substance or structure of the poem, and its increment of irrelevant local substance or texture. I believe that the understanding of the ideal critic has to go even further than that. The final desideratum is an ontological insight, nothing less. I am committed by my title to a representation of criticism as, in the last resort, a speculative exercise. But my secret committal was to speculative in the complete sense of—ontological.

There is nothing especially speculative or ontological in reciting, or even appraising, the logical substance of the poem. This is its prose core—its science perhaps, or its ethics if it seems to have an ideology. Speculative interest asserts itself principally when we ask why we want the logical substance to be compounded with the local substance, the good lean structure with a great volume of texture that does not function. It is the same thing as asking why we want the poem to be what it is.

It has been a rule, having the fewest exceptions, for estheticians and great philosophers to direct their speculations by the way of overstating and overvaluing the logical substance. They are impressed by the apparent obedience of material nature, whether in fact or in art, to definable form or "law" imposed upon it. They like to suppose that in poetry, as in chemistry, everything that figures in the discourse means to be functional, and that the poem is imperfect in the degree that it contains items, whether by accident or intention, which manifest a private independence. It is a bias with which we are entirely familiar, and reflects the extent to which our philosophy hitherto has been impressed by the successes of science in formulating laws which would "govern" their objects. Probably I am here reading the state of mind of yesterday rather than of today. Nevertheless we know it. The world-view which ultimately forms itself in the mind so biassed is that of a world which is rational and intel-ligible. The view is sanguine, and naïve. Hegel's world-view, I think it is agreed, was a subtle version of this, and if so, it was what determined his view of art. He seemed to make the handsomest concession to realism by offering to knowledge a kind of universal which was not restricted to the usual abstracted aspects of the material, but included all aspects, and was a con-crete universal. The concreteness in Hegel's handling was not honestly, or at any rate not fairly, defended. It was always represented as being in process of point-ing up and helping out the universality. He could look at a work of art and report all its substance as almost assimilated to a ruling "idea." But at least Hegel seemed to distinguish what looked like two ultimate sorts of substance there, and stated the central esthetic problem as the problem of relating them. And his writings about art are speculative in the sense that he regarded the work of art not as of great intrinsic value necessarily, but as an object-lesson or discipline in the understanding of the world-process, and as its symbol.

I think of two ways of construing poetry with respect to its ultimate purpose; of which the one is not very handsome nor speculatively interesting, and the other will appear somewhat severe.

The first construction would picture the poet as a sort of epicure, and the poem as something on the order of a Christmas pudding, stuffed with what dainties it will hold. The pastry alone, or it may be the cake, will not serve; the stuffing is wanted too. The values of the poem would be intrinsic, or immediate, and they would include not only the value of the structure but also the incidental values to be found in the texture. If we exchange the pudding for a house, they would include not only the value of the house itself but also the value of the furnishings. In saying intrinsic or immediate, I mean that the poet is fond of the precise objects denoted by the words, and writes the poem for the reason that he likes to dwell upon them. In talking about the main value and the incidental values I mean to recognize the fact that the latter engage the affections just as truly as the former. Poetic discourse therefore would be more agreeable than prose to the epicure or the literally acquisitive man; for prose has but a single value, being about one thing only; its parts have no values of their own, but only instrumental values, which might be reckoned as fractions of the single value proportionate to their contributions to it. The prose is one-valued and the poem is many-valued. Indeed, there will certainly be poems whose texture contains many precious objects, and aggregates a greater value than the structure.

So there would be a comfortable and apparently eligible view that poetry improves on prose because it is a richer diet. It causes five or six pleasures to appear, five or six good things, where one had been before; an alluring consideration for robustious, full-blooded, bourgeois souls. The view will account for much of the poem, if necessary. But it does not account for all of it, and sometimes it accounts for less than at other times.

The most impressive reason for the bolder view of art, the speculative one, is the existence of the "pure," or "abstractionist," or non-representational works of art; though these will probably occur to us in other arts than poetry. There is at least one art, music, whose works are all of this sort. Tones are not words, they have no direct semantical function, and by themselves they mean nothing. But they combine to make brilliant phrases, harmonies, and compositions. In these compositions it is probable that the distinction between structure or functional content, on the one hand, and texture or local variation and departure, on the other, is even more determinate than in an impure art like poetry. The world of tones seems perfectly inhuman and impracticable; there is no specific field of experience "about which" music is telling us. Yet we know that music is powerfully affective. I take my own musical feelings, and those attested by other audients, as the sufficient index to some overwhelming human importance which the musical object has for us. At the same time it would be useless to ask the feelings precisely what they felt; we must ask the critic. The safest policy is to take the simplest construction, and try to improvise as little fiction as possible. Music is not music, I think, until we grasp its effects both in structure and in texture. As we grow in musical understanding the structures become always more elaborate and sustained, and the texture which interrupts them and sometimes imperils them becomes more bold and unpredictable. We can agree in saying about the works of music that these are musical structures, and they are richly textured; we can identify these elements, and perhaps precisely. To what then do our feelings respond? To music as structural composition itself; to music as manifesting the structural principles of the world; to modes of structure which we feel to be ontologically possible, or even probable. Schopenhauer construed music very much in that sense. Probably it will occur to us that musical compositions bear close analogy therefore to operations in pure mathematics. The mathematicians confess that their constructions are "non-existential"; meaning, as I take it, that the constructions testify with assurance only to the structural principles, in the light of which they are possible but may not be actual, or if they are actual may not be useful. This would define the mathematical operations as speculative: as motivated by an interest so generalized and so elemental that no word short of ontological will describe it.

But if music and mathematics have this much in common, they differ sharply in their respective world-views or ontological biasses. That of music, with its prodigious display of texture, seems the better informed about the nature of the world, the more realistic, the less naive. Perhaps the difference is between two ontological educations. But I should be inclined to imagine it as rising back of that point: in two ontological temperaments.

There are also, operating a little less successfully so far as the indexical evidences would indicate, the abstractionist paintings, of many schools, and perhaps also works of sculpture; and there is architecture. These arts have tried to abandon direct representational intention almost as heroically as music. They exist in their own materials and indicate no other specific materials; structures of color, light, space, stone—the cheapest of materials. They too can symbolize nothing of value unless it is structure or composition itself. But that is precisely the act which denotes will and intelligence; which becomes the act of fuller intelligence if it carefully accompanies its structures with their material textures; for then it understands better the ontological nature of materials.

Cuckoo, cuckoo: O word of fear,
Unpleasing to a married ear!

WINTER. When icicles hang by the wall,
And Dick the shepherd blows his nail,
And Tom bears logs into the hall,
And milk comes frozen home in pail,
When blood is nipp'd and ways be foul,
Then nightly sings the staring owl,
Tu-who;
Tu-whit, tu-who, a merry note,
While greasy Joan doth keel the pot.

When all aloud the wind doth blow,
And coughing drowns the parson's saw,
And birds sit brooding in the snow,
And Marian's nose looks red and raw,
When roasted crabs hiss in the bowl,
Then nightly sings the staring owl,
Tu-who;
Tu-whit, tu-who, a merry note,
While greasy Joan doth keel the pot.

ARM. The words of Mercury are harsh after the
songs of Apollo. You that way,—we this way.
(*Exeunt.*)

The feeling-index registers such strong approval of
this episode that a critic with ambition is obliged to

account for it. He can scarcely account for it in terms of the weight of its contents severally.

At first glance Shakespeare has provided only a pleasant little caricature of the old-fashioned (to us, medieval) debate between personified characters. It is easygoing, like nonsense; no labor is lost here. Each party speaks two stanzas and concludes both stanzas with the refrain about his bird, the cuckoo or the owl. There is next to no generalized argument, or dialectic proper. Each argues by citing his characteristic exhibits. In the first stanza Spring cites some flowers; in the second stanza, some business by country persons, with interpolation of some birds that make love. Winter in both his stanzas cites the country business of the season. In the refrain the cuckoo, Spring's symbol, is used to refer the love-making to more than the birds; and this repeats itself, though it is naughty. The owl is only a nominal symbol for Winter, an "emblem" that is not very emblematic, but the refrain manages another reference to the kitchen, and repeats itself, as if Winter's pleasures focussed in the kitchen.

In this poem texture is not very brilliant, but it eclipses structure. The argument, we would say in academic language, is concerned with "the relative advantages of Spring and Winter." The only logical determinateness this structure has is the good coordination of the items cited by Spring as being really items peculiar to Spring, and of the Winter items as peculiar to Winter. The symbolic refrains look like summary or master items, but they seem to be a little more than summary and in fact to mean a little more than they say. The argument is trifling on the whole, and the texture from the point of view of felt human importance lacks decided energy; both which observations are to be made, and most precisely, of how many famous lyrics, especially those before that earnest and self-conscious nineteenth century! The value of the poem is greater than the value of its parts: that is what the critic is up against.

Unquestionably it is possible to assemble very fine structures out of ordinary materials. The good critic will study the poet's technique, in confidence that here the structural principles will be discovered at home. In this study he will find as much range for his activities as he desires.

Especially must he study the metrics, and their implications for structural composition. In this poem I think the critic ought to make good capital of the contrast between the amateurishness of the pleasant discourse as meaning and the hard determinate form of it phonetically. The meter on the whole is out of relation to the meaning of the poem, or to anything else specifically; it is a musical material of low grade, but plastic and only slightly resistant material, and its presence in every poem is that of an abstractionist element that belongs to the art.

And here I will suggest another analogy, this one between Shakespeare's poem and some ordinary specimen of painting. It does not matter how old-fashioned or representational the painting is, we shall all, if we are instructed in the tradition of this art, require it to exhibit along with its represented object an abstract design in terms of pure physical balance or symmetry. We sense rather than measure the success of this design, but it is as if we had drawn a horizontal axis and a vertical axis through the center of the picture, and required the painted masses to balance with respect to each of these two axes. This is an over-simple statement of a structural requirement by which the same details function in two worlds that are different, and that do not correlate with each other. If the painting is of the Holy Family, we might say that this object has a drama, or an economy, of its own; but that the physical masses which compose it must enter also into another economy, that of abstract design; and that the value of any unit mass for the one economy bears no relation to its value for the other. The painting is of great ontological interest because it embodies this special dimension of abstract form. And turning to the poem, we should find that its represented "meaning" is analogous to the represented object in the painting, while its meter is analogous to the pure design.

A number of fascinating speculative considerations must follow upon this discovery. They will have to do with the most fundamental laws of this world's structure. They will be profoundly ontological, though I do not mean that they must be ontological in some recondite sense; ontological in such a homely and compelling sense that perhaps a child might intuit the principles which the critic will arrive at analytically, and with much labor.

I must stop at this point, since I am desired not so much to anticipate the critic as to present him. In conclusion I will remark that the critic will doubtless work empirically, and set up his philosophy only as the drift of his findings will compel him. But ultimately he will be compelled. He will have to subscribe to an ontology. If he is a sound critic his ontology will be that of his poets; and what is that? I suggest that the poetic world-view is Aristotelian and "realistic" rather than Platonic and "idealistic." He cannot follow the poets and still conceive himself as inhabiting the rational or "tidy" universe that is supposed by the scientists.

CRITICISM IN A MASS SOCIETY

· By W. H. AUDEN ·

Criticism in a Mass Society

WE are frequently and correctly told that one of the most precious privileges of a democratic state is the right to free self-criticism. If we care, then, about the preservation of that democracy, our first duty is to discover how this right is, in fact, exercised. It will not take us long to discover that in a modern society, whatever its political form, the great majority prefer opinion to knowledge, and passively allow the former to be imposed upon them by a centralized few—I need only mention as an example the influence of the Sunday book supplements of the newspapers upon our public libraries.

If we are concerned, as I think we should be, at this trend, we shall accomplish nothing by cries of lamentation or superior sneers; we cannot hope to effect any reform unless we can discover, firstly, what it is in the structure of our society that makes for this state of affairs, secondly, how far the molding of the opinions of the few by the many is inevitable, and then what steps it is possible to take within the inevitable to minimize its dangers and take advantage of its possibilities.

1. There are two types of society: closed societies and open.

2. All human societies begin by being of the closed type, but, except when they have stagnated or died, they have always evolved toward an ever more and more open type. Up until the industrial revolution this evolution was so gradual as hardly to be perceptible within the life-span of an individual, but since then the rate of development has ever increasingly accelerated.

3. The evolutionary process is complicated by the fact that different sections of the community progress toward the open society at different speeds. At any given point in history there are classes for whom economic, political, and cultural advantages make society relatively open, and, vice versa, those for whom similar disadvantages make it relatively closed, but in comparing one historical epoch with its preceding one, all classes are seen to have made some evolution in the same direction.

4. When we use the word democracy we do not or should not mean any particular form of political structure; such matters are secondary. What we mean or ought to mean is the completely open society.

5. The technical obstacles to this have been overcome. What is holding us back is the failure of totalitarians and democrats alike to realize how open society has already physically become, so that we continue to apply habits of mind which were more or less adequate to the relatively closed society of the eighteenth century to an open society which demands completely new

ones. The failure of the human race to acquire the habits that an open society demands if it is to function properly, is leading an increasing number of people to the conclusion that an open society is impossible, and that, therefore, the only escape from economic and spiritual disaster is to return as quickly as possible to a closed type of society. But social evolution, fortunately or unfortunately, is irreversible. A mechanized and differentiated closed society is a self-contradiction. We have in fact no choice at all; we have to adapt ourselves to an open society or perish.

No human community of course has ever been completely closed, and none probably will ever be completely open, but from the researches of anthropologists and historians, we can construct a Platonic idea of both.

Ideally, a closed society is physically segregated, economically autonomous and without cultural contact with other communities. Occupationally it is undifferentiated; everyone does the same kind of work, agriculture, fishing, hunting, etc.; such differences as exist are based on biological differences of sex and age. In the education of the young there is no distinction between vocational or technical and cultural or moral training; all activities are governed by tradition; the right thing to do is inseparable from the right way of doing it (an identity found today only in compulsion neurosis). Education ends with puberty; to be mature means to be socially normal. In contrast to its primitive economy, the character type imposed on all its members is extremely specialized and may vary fantastically from one closed society to another; the Arapesh type, for example, is cooperative and pacific, the Dobu type is a paranoiac. Aberrant individuals who fail to be conditioned must become either hermits or saboteurs. Art as a means to satisfy internal psychic needs and science as a means to satisfy external material needs, are included in an undifferentiated complex of communal activities; it is not realized that an incantatory curse is intrinsically different from a stab with a knife.

The religion by which it lives is polytheistic: little or no distinction is drawn between the particular and the universal, the sign and its signification. In its taboos and regulations it has not learned to distinguish between propositions or statements which can be proved true or false by immediate experiment, and presuppositions or professions of faith. Since the individual is scarcely differentiated from the whole and technique is primitive, freedom consists largely in a consciousness of causal necessity either in the form of the forces of nature or of the social pressures of tradition, and to only a very slight degree in a consciousness of logical necessity. The motto of such a society is that of the trolls in Peer Gynt—to thyself be enough.

The ideal open society on the other hand would know no physical, economic or cultural frontiers. Conscious both of what it possessed and what it lacked, it would exchange freely with all others. Occupationally specialized, the range of occupations to choose from would be so wide that there would be no one, however exceptional his nature, who could not find his genuine vocation. Such a community would be tolerant because it found every kind of person useful, and its members socially responsible because conscious of being needed.

Mechanized, it would have conquered nature but would recognize that conquest for what it is—not the abolition of necessity, but the transformation of much of the external causal necessity of matter into the internal logical necessity of moral decision.

The concept of normality would have disappeared, for, since an open society requires open individuals, maturity would be regarded as an ideal goal that is never reached. The aim of education would be to assist the child who is born as a closed system of reflex responses to grow up into an adult who is open to the degree to which he ceases to be merely accessory to his position and becomes aware of who he is and what he really wants. For we do not essentially change as we grow up; the difference between the child and the adult is that the former is not conscious of his destiny and the latter is. His motto is that of the human beings in Peer Gynt—to thyself be true.

Far as we are and perhaps always must be from realizing this in our social life, in our cultural and intellectual life we have moved a long way toward it. Instead of working within the limits of one regional or national esthetic tradition, the modern artist works with a consciousness of all the cultural productions, not only of the whole world of his day, but also of the whole historical past. Thus one sculptor may be influenced by the forms of electrical machinery, another by African masks, another by Donatello and so on. The three greatest influences on my own work have been, I think, Dante, Langland, and Pope.

If we talk of tradition today, we no longer mean what the eighteenth century meant, a way of working handed down from one generation to the next; we mean a consciousness of the whole of the past in the present. Originality no longer means a slight personal modification of one's immediate predecessors, as for example the music of Haydn or Schubert differs from that of Mozart; it means the capacity to find in any other work of any date or locality clues for the treatment of one's own personal subject matter. Stravinsky and Picasso are good example of artists who at different times have made personal modifications of entirely different techniques.

Over against this cultural unity of time and space, however, stands the increasing uniqueness in modern life of the individual's social position. When I hear critics talk of an American art, I am at a loss to know which America they mean; the America of a Negro janitor in the Bronx is almost as different from the

America of a prosperous white farmer in Wisconsin as France is from China.

The importance that criticism and belles-lettres take today can be understood only if we recognize these two characteristics of our society: the tendency toward individuation of experience, and the change in the meaning of the word tradition.

The contemporary critic has two primary tasks. Firstly he must show the individual that though he is unique he has also much in common with all other individuals, that each life is, to use a chemical metaphor, an isomorph of a general human life and then must teach him how to see the relevance to his own experience of works of art which deal with experiences apparently strange to him; so that, for example, the coal miner in Pennsylvania can learn to see himself in terms of the world of Ronald Firbank, and an Anglican bishop find in *The Grapes of Wrath* a parable of his diocesan problems.

And secondly the critic must attempt to spread a knowledge of past cultures so that his audience may be as aware of them as the artist himself, not only simply in order to appreciate the latter, but because the situation of all individuals, artist and audience alike, in an open society is such that the only check on authoritarian control by the few, whether in matters of esthetic taste or political choice, is the knowledge of the many. We cannot of course all be experts in everything; we are always governed, and I hope willingly, by those whom we believe to be expert; but our society has already reached a point in its development where the expert can be recognized only by an educated judgment. The standard demanded of the man in the street (and outside our own special field, we are all men in the street) rises with every generation.

This cannot be emphasized too strongly. In earlier phases of social development a man could be a member of a group (i.e., not, in our sense, an individual), and yet be a person; he could be accessory to his position because the latter was a real necessity, and by virtue of being a necessity, could make him free. Today a man has only two choices: he can be consciously passive or consciously active. He can accept deliberately or reject deliberately, but he must decide because his position in life is no longer a real necessity; he could be different if he chose. The necessity that can make him free is no longer his position as such, but the necessity of choosing to accept or reject it. To be unconscious is to be neither an individual nor a person, but a mathematical integer in something called the Public which has no real existence.

This is, alas, what only too often happens. We have heard much in the last twenty years of the separation of the modern artist from the crowd, of how modern art is unintelligible to the average man, and it is commonly but falsely supposed that this is because the artist is a special case. In my opinion, on the contrary, the lack of communication between artist and audience proves the lack of communication between all men; a work of art only unmasks the lack which is common to us all, but which we normally manage to gloss over with every trick and convention of conversation; men are now only individuals who can form collective masses but not communities.

One common reaction to this is to place responsibility for our defects upon fate, by saying that we are living in an age of transition, implying that if only we are patiently passive our faults will disappear of themselves when the new order has stabilized itself. This is a false and dangerous way of stating a valuable truth; perhaps the only decisive advantage we possess over our ancestors is a historical knowledge which enables us to see that all ages are ages of transition. This realization robs us of false hopes, of believing, if we are fortunate, that the Absolute Idea has been at last historically realized, or of expecting, if we are unfortunate, a millennium around the corner. At the same time it should keep us from despair; no error is final.

Whatever our nationality, occupation, or beliefs, we are all agreed on one thing; that the times through which we are now living mark the end of a period which, for convenience, we can say began with the Renaissance. We are all consciously or unconsciously seeking some form of catholic unity to correct the moral, artistic, and political chaos that has resulted from an over-development of protestant diversity (using these terms in their widest sense). Our differences, and they are vital, are as to the essential nature of that unity and the form which it should take. The cohesion of a society is secured by a mixture of three factors, community of actions, community of faith and beliefs, and coercion by those who possess the means of exercising it. In a differentiated society like our own, the first factor has in large measure disappeared. If we are agreed that the third should be as small an influence as possible, we must examine the second very carefully.

I have used two words, faith and belief, to describe two different forms of assent: assent to presuppositions which cannot be immediately proved true or false, as, for example, science presupposes that the world of nature exists; and assent to propositions that can be experimentally tested, e.g., the proposition that water boils at one hundred degrees centigrade. In proportion as a society is closed and traditional it tends to regard all propositions as presuppositions and so to discourage initiative and research because it fears the destruction of its fundamental assumptions. Conversely, in proportion as a society becomes open and experimental it is in danger of denying the necessity of making any presuppositions at all. Further, in any society where there is a struggle for the power of control, the Ins will tend to preach a static monism which identifies the absolute and universal with their own concrete and particular, while the Outs, in exposing this ideological pretension, will tend toward a relative dualism which denies or ignores absolutes altogether. This is dangerous. The statement, "Man is a fallen creature with a natural bias to do evil," and the statement, "Men are good by nature and made bad by society," are both presuppositions, but it is not an academic question to which one we give assent. If, as I do, you assent to the first, your art and politics will be very different from what they will be if you assent, like Rousseau or Whitman, to the second.

The history of art and esthetic criticism is an excellent field for the study of these difficulties. In the first place, since the breakdown of patronage in the eighteenth century, the artist has been the extreme case of the free individual, the one for whom, more than for any other, society has become open and untraditional; and in the second place, since art by its nature is a shared, a catholic, activity, he is the first to feel the consequences of a lack of common beliefs, and the first to seek a common basis for human unity.

The Renaissance broke the subordination of all other intellectual fields to that of theology, and assumed the autonomy of each. The artists of the Renaissance sought canons of esthetic judgment which should be independent and self-supporting, and believed that they had found them in the classics, forgetting that the esthetics of the Greeks were inseparable from social habits and religious beliefs which they themselves did not share. The attempt to make esthetics an autonomous province resulted in academic esthetics, the substitution of the pedant for the priest.

The romantic reaction defied the pedant in the name of liberty for the imaginative original genius, but thereby only accentuated the two great esthetic problems, the problem of communication and the problem of value. For the absolutely unique would be absolutely incommunicable; and unless, in some respects, all men are alike, that is, unoriginal, all taste is purely personal. Thus even the most romantic artists have attempted to justify their art by correspondence to a Nature which all can recognize.

Some assumed that the only point of agreement between individuals lay in the similarity of their sense perceptions and became "realists," i.e., they attempted to give an exact description of phenomenal facts. Unfortunately, since the facts are infinite in number and their selection is not performed by the sense organs themselves, unless we assume more than this, such art must logically end in manufacturing nature herself; it will not be enough to paint a lake, one will have to make one.

Others turned to the unconscious and instinctive as a basis of unity and became "surrealists." Unfortunately again, since one cannot create without becoming conscious of so doing, unless we assume more than this, such art must end in silent, unconscious telepathy.

Esthetics since the last war has therefore been forced to take seriously the problem of belief in art. Some, like Dr. I. A. Richards, have subordinated esthetics to psychology. A poem organizes our emotional attitudes; it is the efficiency of this organization, not the truth or falsehood of the belief expressed, that determines the esthetic value of the poem. In admitting that there is such a thing as a good poem or a bad poem, it demands an impersonal objective standard for judging the quality of the organization achieved. If I understand Dr. Richards rightly, this standard is to be found not in ethics or metaphysics or religion but in psychology. Now psychology, considered in isolation from other fields, is either a descriptive account of the result of introspection, or a practical science whose values are pragmatic; i.e., that is valuable which achieves most successfully a predetermined end. What is the end that Dr. Richards' psychology assumes is given? I suspect that it is truth, righteousness and peace; I hope so. But suppose it is not? Then the psychological approach must end, as the Freudian psychology does, in making local, social, and historical conditions the criteria of normality against which every deviation is neurotic; art then becomes only a circuitous route to "Honor, power, glory and the love of women." This either denies any esthetic values at all, or makes the latter in direct proportion to popular appeal, and the appreciation of any art of another period impossible. This is to subordinate esthetics to politics and, though it may be the real view of the militant marxist, it is certainly not what Dr. Richards intends.

In seeking to account for the experience of all readers of poetry, that the metaphysical beliefs expressed in a poem are not solely decisive in our assessment of its value, he denies them any rôle at all. This is going too far. What he really establishes is the interdependence of belief and expression of belief, the Word and the Flesh, Faith and Works, that what we think cannot be isolated from what we say and do. False beliefs in fact lead to bad poetry, and bad poetry leads to a falsification of belief. Thus in his poem "Trees," a false esthetic has caused Joyce Kilmer to make statements which even from his own Catholic standpoint are heretical, while a false conception of human nature led Thomas Wolfe to write the grandiose rubbish he mistook for great prose.

Dr. Richards once said that *The Waste Land* marked the severance of poetry from all beliefs. This seems to me an inaccurate description. The poem is *about* the absence of belief and its very unpleasant consequences; it implies throughout a passionate belief in damnation: that to be without belief is to be lost. I cannot see how those who do not share this belief, those who think that truth is relative or pragmatic, can regard the poem as anything but an interesting case history of Mr. Eliot's neurotic state of mind.

The combination of this acceptance of all values as relative with the social conditions of a modern industrial society makes confusion worse confounded. The machine has destroyed tradition in the old sense and the refusal to replace it by absolute presuppositions deliberately chosen and consciously held is leading us to disaster. In the first place when tradition disappears so does popular taste; in saying that he can sell anything, the advertiser is admitting that there is no such thing as the taste of the man in the street: and in the second, the centralization of an industrial society places the dictatorship of taste in the hands of a very small group of people. If we are ever to achieve anything remotely resembling a democratic culture, we must all begin by admitting the fact of this dictatorship, and the critics themselves must accept their responsibility and not mislead the public.

Let me take as an illustration of irresponsibility a review by a distinguished American critic. I choose this example because the critic who wrote it is more fortunate than most in not having to be a publisher's lackey and because though I have not read the novel I think that I should probably agree with his verdict.

"As one whose heart is coated, I fear, with a thick daubing of common clay, I see in *The* Voyage a beguiling romance and not a piece of profound symbolism. Though far less oracular and pretentious than Mr. Morgan's other novels, it is still fairly fancy for gross tastes like my own."

Why does he really find Mr. Morgan pretentious? Because his sensibility is too trained to be deceived. But this is not the reason he gives. He pretends he is just a plain man who can see through all that; in other words it is the untrained intellect and sensibility that alone can make sound critical judgments. This is irresponsible, for he knows as well as anyone that it is precisely the hearts daubed with clay and the gross taste that fall for the genteel and the bogusly spiritual. Certainly we are all common clay and should admit the fact—but with shame, not pride. What the critic ought to say is: "Remember that like you and everyone else I am a weak fallible creature who will often make false judgments; and therefore you must not take everything I say as gospel. I as a reviewer promise to do my best to overcome my natural laziness and wooly-mindedness, and you who read me must try to do the same."

This would be a beginning, but a great deal more should be expected. Not only should the critic realize the necessity of coordinating his esthetic values with values in all other spheres of life, but he has a duty in a democracy to tell the public what they are. If I am to trust a reviewer's judgment upon a book I have not read, I want to know among other things his philosophical beliefs. If I find, for instance, that he believes in automatic progress I shall no more trust him than I would trust a philosopher who liked Brahms or Shelley.

I do not, of course, mean to suggest that the State or anyone else should decree an orthodoxy to which all critics must conform or forever hold their peace, but only that, since life does not exist in a series of autonomous departments, esthetic values do not nourish themselves, and that the critic who does not realize this will be a bad critic who misleads the public and at best can only be right on occasions by luck.

Earlier in this lecture I suggested that democracy and fascism are disagreed, not upon the need for cultural unity, but on its nature and form. I would summarize these differences thus.

SOCIAL DEMOCRACY	FASCISM
1. We cannot live without believing certain values to be absolute. These values exist, though our knowledge of them is always imperfect, distorted by the limitations of our historical position and our personal character. However, if but only if we realize this, our knowledge can improve.	The masses cannot live without believing certain values to be absolute. Such values, however, do not exist; therefore the state must coerce the masses into accepting as absolute what in fact are myths. The choice of myth is dictated by its pragmatic value as conceived by the leaders of the state.
2. Because the existence of absolutes implies the unity of truth, the truths arrived at in different fields cannot ultimately conflict. All the arts and	Because the nonexistence of absolutes implies the relativity of truth, the truths arrived at in different fields must ultimately conflict. Unity and sta-

sciences therefore must be assumed to be of equal value, isomorphs of one common cooperative task, and no one of these must be subordinated to another.

bility therefore can be achieved only under social pressure. Since it is the politician who commands the means of pressure, all the other arts and sciences must be subordinated to the political.

3. Man is not, as the romantics imagined, good by nature. Men are equal not in their capacities and virtues but in their natural bias toward evil. No individual or class, therefore, however superior in intellect or character to the rest, can claim an absolute right to impose its view of the good upon them. Government must be democratic, the people must have a right to make their own mistakes and to suffer for them, because no one is free from error.

All men are not as the romantics imagined good by nature, nor are they equal. Further, since the political field is the determining one and the first element in political goodness is the capacity to exercise power, that capacity takes precedence over all others in defining the Good. The majority are bad, but a few are good and have therefore a right to direct the rest. Government must be authoritarian; the people must be protected from the consequences of their own mistakes by those who cannot err.

4. To deny to those who are in fact the élite of their age the right to impose their authority by force, does not deny their obligation to educate and persuade. Responsibility is in direct proportion to capacity.

The power to exercise authority implies an obligation to do so.

If we accept the democratic assumptions what consequences will follow in the field of criticism?

1. The critic who assumes that absolute values exist but that our knowledge of them is always imperfect

will judge a work of art by the degree to which it transcends the artist's personal and historical limitations, but he will not expect such transcendence ever to be complete, either in the artist or himself. He will equip himself with social and historical knowledge in order to overcome his own prejudices and to help the reader to see, through all the apparent differences in the technique and subject matter of great works, their underlying unity. He will be suspicious of all that is partisan, naturalistic, and personal, and of all such antitheses as Traditional versus Modern.

2. Assuming the unity of truth he will realize the interdependence of ethics, politics, science, esthetics, etc. and do his best to acquire as all-round a culture as possible. Assuming the equal value of these fields, he will in judging a book attempt to keep them all in mind without being dominated by any one of them. He will try to avoid, for example, both the puritanical attitude of the bourgeois censor of morals and the nihilist attitude of the bohemian who ignores or denies the effect of moral values upon works of art and the moral influence which they do in fact exert. Slogans like Art for Art's Sake or Art for Politics' Sake will be equally objectionable to him.

3. Admitting original sin, he will not believe in his own infallibility, or cause others to believe in it. He will be as chary of utterly condemning a book as of acclaiming it a masterpiece. He will flatter neither the

masses by assuring them that what is popular must be good nor the highbrow by assuring them that what is *avantgarde* must be superior. Further he will conceive of art, like life, as being a self-discipline rather than a self-expression. Like Henry James he will regard "Clumsy life at her stupid work" as something to be mastered and controlled. He will see artistic freedom and personality as dependent upon the voluntary acceptance of limitations, which alone are strong enough to test the genuine intensity of the original creative impulse; he will distrust the formless, the expansive, the unfinished, and the casual.

4. Accepting his responsibility, he will see his position of influence as an accident, an inheritance which he does not deserve and which he is incompetent to administer. For though it is absolutely required of a man that he should intend to help others, the power to do so is outside his control. No man can guarantee the effect upon others of the acts he does with the intention of helping them. Indeed all he knows for certain is that, since his actions are never perfect, he must always do others harm, so that the final aim of every critic and teacher must be to persuade others to do without him, to realize that the gifts of the spirit are never to be had at second hand.

Thus no critic or teacher must deceive himself or others by pretending that he criticizes for their sake; he has no right either to criticize or teach unless he can say: "I do this, whatever its effects, because I cannot help doing it."

In the last analysis every act of critical judgment, like every other act in life, like life itself, rests on a decision, a wager which is irrevocable and in a sense absurd. But unless we have the courage and faith to take such decisions with full recognition of their arbitrary and conditional character, nothing can save us, individually or collectively, now or at any other time, from a dictatorship which we shall regret. Dictatorship has been defined as a state where everything that is not obligatory is forbidden, and in that sense man has always lived under a dictatorship and always will. Our only choice lies between an external and false necessity passively accepted and an internal necessity consciously decided, but that is the difference between slavery and freedom.